AURELIE LITYNSKI

100

IDEAS

FOR A
POSITIVE
WORK
CULTURE

III Clink
Street

To those who believe that work can be a place of growth, happiness, and purpose - may this book inspire you!

EXPLORE THE CHAPTERS

CHAPTER 9

MASTERING STRESS & BOOSTING FOCUS..215

CHAPTER 10

FOSTERING A FEELING OF ACHIEVEMENT 249

HAPPY REVIEWS

"This book combines deep expertise with actionable insights to boost morale, engagement, and productivity—essential for modern workplaces!"
Nir Eyal – Bestselling author of "Indistractable: How to Control Your Attention and Choose Your Life"

"Aurelie Litynski's 100 Ideas for a Positive Work Culture is exactly what today's workplaces need. As happiness in the workplace becomes a key driver of sustainable business success, this book offers practical, tested tips to create and sustain positive, productive teams. These 100 ideas are a must-have for anyone looking to improve workplace life—benefiting employees, customers, and organizations alike."
Prof. John F. Helliwell – Vancouver School of Economics, University of British Columbia. Editor, World Happiness Report

---

"One of the significant challenges in promoting happiness in the workplace is how to synthesize the vast evidence base into useful practical tips for practitioners and leaders. With her rich expertise in the practice of well-being in all its dimensions: physical, social, and psychological, Aurelie has developed a brilliant collection of 100 practices to enhance workplace well-being and transform your team's culture!"
Dr. K. Vish Viswanath – Lee Kum Kee Professor of Health Communication, Harvard T.H. Chan School of Public Health

---

"This book is both practical and aspirational! It's an excellent guide for developing employees' human skills and creating actionable training strategies that foster a truly human-centric company culture. A valuable resource for any Learning & Development professional committed to meaningful growth."
Joti Joseph – Head People and Organisational Development, Vontobel

---

"Aurelie Litynski has consistently empowered our teams with her expertise, infectious positivity, and profound insight into workplace dynamics. Her book serves as a vital resource for leaders dedicated to reshaping workplace culture and fostering high-performing teams. Featuring 100 practical, inspiring, and actionable ideas, it stands as a compelling guide for driving positive transformation."

Panos Drakoulas – VP OUS Commercial, Medtronic

"This book is my trusted companion and will stay close to my desk as a go-to guide. I love the practical examples and exercises that inspire me to reflect and take action. It's an empowering roadmap to creating a positive and sustainable work culture, which you can tailor to your own challenges and opportunities. I highly recommend it!"

Laura Jollit – Creative Events Producer and Marketing Specialist, Cognizant Netcentric

"If you're striving to create a workplace that radiates positivity, creativity, and inspiration, this is the book you've been waiting for. Packed with over 100 practical and enjoyable ideas, this book makes creating a happier environment feel refreshingly doable, no matter where you're starting from. This isn't just another book about workplace culture—it's a warm, actionable, and empowering guide that will inspire you to make happiness a cornerstone of your leadership or team. Dive in, try it out, and watch your workplace transform into a space where everyone thrives. A must-read for anyone passionate about building better workplaces!"

Marco Di Sante – General Manager Opella Healthcare Switzerland and Austria

"Aurelie is the embodiment of workplace happiness that everyone truly deserves. This book is an essential guide on your journey toward building a positive work culture."

Joe Justice – Founder of WIKISPEED and Agile Business Institute, Author of Scrum Master, Founder of agile@tesla

HOW TO READ THIS BOOK

This book isn't just another business book!

It's a practical guide containing 100 powerful ideas that will revolutionize workplace dynamics. Before anything, keep in mind that you don't need to read the pages in strict order – chart your own journey.

The 100 ideas are organized into ten different topics with the aim of helping you cultivate a positive work culture. I encourage you to keep this guide handy so you can jump to the specific chapter you need for support and find inspiration.

Drawing from my years of experience supporting companies around the world, I've gathered innovative initiatives, learned practical tools, and collected success stories. In my work leading webinars, workshops, or inspirational talks for countless teams, I usually provide a toolbox of hands-on tools related to the session's topic, whether it's about positive psychology, emotional intelligence, stress management, or leadership. These toolboxes often become highlights of the sessions, sparking positivity and creating lasting changes in team dynamics. Inspired by feedback from participants who found them easy to implement and expressed a desire for more, I created this guide – a comprehensive toolbox for fostering positivity in the workplace and offering strategies for individuals, teams, and organizations alike.

Before you dive in, here's how to get the most out of this book.

➡ Start by reading the first three chapters to get a foundational understanding of positive work culture, emotions at work, and well-being.

➡ Then, hop to whichever chapter speaks to you. Feeling stressed? Jump to Chapter 9. Want to build stronger workplace relationships? Chapter 5 has you covered!

➡ Each chapter contains a variety of initiatives – some for individuals, others for teams or leaders – so feel free to mix and match those that work best for your unique situation. The lengths and amount of ideas will vary depending on the chapter, allowing you to choose according to your time and goals.

→ As you go through the 100 ideas, highlight the ones that resonate the most with you so you can get back to them when you're ready for some action!

→ You will find at the end of each chapter a section to take action, to reflect on the topic, and to write your own notes.

→ The book also includes Expert Corners, Fact Corners, and interviews with inspiring leaders who have made significant contributions to fostering a positive work culture, providing real-life business examples.

→ To keep the guide interactive and up-to-date, I have created a single QR code for you to scan and access additional examples. Once you have scanned this code, you can select the chapter for which you want more resources, whether it's videos, articles, or pictures that support the content. These add-ons will be regularly updated, so make sure to check them once in a while.

Throughout the book, scan the QR code at the end of each chapter to access expert insights, additional resources, videos, articles, and downloadable content:

While each chapter and topic could be expanded into its own book, my goal is to provide you with key insights into the core principles of each topic. I encourage you to explore each section further, if needed, using the extra resources linked via the QR code and by following the experts and leaders mentioned.

This book is for everyone, not just senior management. Even if you're not leading a team, you can implement many ideas for yourself and, on top of that, positively influence your manager and colleagues by suggesting initiatives that benefit your whole team. Be inspired to adapt them to your situation, industry, seniority level, and work style. Most of the initiatives are adaptable to both remote and office-based work.

Should you implement all 100 ideas? Most probably not. It would be overkill! Select the ones that resonate for you and your team. Start by trying some, adapt if needed, and implement step by step!

Keep this guide handy – it's your go-to toolbox to foster a positive work culture.

Just grab an idea and start bringing positivity into your workplace, one initiative at a time. Let's build workplaces where everyone thrives!

1

IT STARTS
WITH YOU

The Importance of Fostering a Positive Work Culture in Companies

It's no secret that having a solid strategy and a team of talented individuals are key components to a successful business. However, it's important to recognize that a positive and strong company culture is equally crucial. Without it, even the best ideas and efforts may not reach their full potential, leaving room for possible setbacks and challenges.

Everyone in the organization contributes to the culture, from top leadership to entry-level employees. While the company's structure, values, and strategy lay the groundwork, its culture is profoundly influenced by all employees, particularly through behaviors, mindset, and attitude.

Fostering a positive work culture is fundamental in today's fast-paced business world. Companies are constantly seeking strategies to enhance productivity and achieve their goals. However, one aspect that is often overlooked is employee happiness and well-being. By prioritizing employees' positive experiences and supporting their personal growth, organizations can boost engagement, reduce burnout, and improve overall business outcomes.

A positive work culture is not about avoiding conflict or being positive every day.

It's about creating an environment where employees feel supported, safe, valued, motivated, respected, appreciated, and empowered to grow, finding meaning and purpose in their roles. It's also about providing constructive ways to manage and resolve conflicts.

It's a constant work in progress that requires dedication and commitment from every level of the organization.

In this chapter, we will begin by exploring the significance of employee happiness in the workplace and how it differs from employee engagement. You will learn what is essential for you to feel good in your job, along with practical tips to enhance your own happiness at work. We will also introduce various factors that contribute to a positive work culture, which you can explore further in the upcoming chapters to foster a more productive and successful team dynamic.

Now, let's talk about happiness!

Ask yourself: Do you prioritize your own happiness in your personal life?

Most of us do, right?

So why don't we prioritize it in the workplace?

It's well-established by experts that happiness at work boosts motivation, engagement, and productivity, and it often goes hand in hand with stronger interpersonal relationships, including trust. For more insights, check the upcoming "Fact Corner" section.

Trust is a key element in building a positive work culture, yet it can be hard to cultivate when we're not feeling our best or don't get along with others at work. It's crucial to create an environment where team happiness is a fundamental part of the culture. The happiness of employees plays a key role in shaping the culture, and a positive culture, in turn, boosts employee well-being – creating a continuous, reinforcing cycle.

Here are some compelling facts that highlight the benefits of fostering a positive team culture:

➡ **Happier employees work better!**

They are more creative, engaged, and motivated. Consequently, they perform better![1]

➡ **Happiness isn't the *result* of success – it's the *cause* of it.**

In a positive state, your brain performs 31% better than in a negative, neutral or stressed state[2]. When individuals operate in a positive mental state, it enhances their brain's performance and productivity. Shawn Achor, researcher and *New York Times* best-selling author, calls it "The Happiness Advantage": the importance of positivity and happiness in achieving success.

➡ **Employee well-being is positively correlated with the company's performance.[3]**

Lower absenteeism rates, higher levels of productivity, increased employee retention, and customer loyalty ultimately lead to im-proved financial performance and increased shareholder value.

➡ **Happy employees = happy teams = happy customers = happy company**

Equation adapted from "The Service Profit Chain Model"[4]

Leading companies link profit and growth to loyalty, satisfaction, and value. Employee satisfaction drives productivity and service quality, which, in turn, lead to customer satisfaction and loyalty. This ultimately contributes to the company's profit and growth— an approach known as the Service Profit Chain.

Employees' Engagement = Employees' Happiness?

In my work with executives to transform their team's culture into a happier and more productive one, many leaders have expressed skepticism about discussing happiness within their teams. I've heard remarks like, *"I cannot bring up the subject of happiness with my team,"* or *"It's not a serious topic for the company to discuss,"* and even *"Happiness is not business-related – we prefer to talk about engagement; it sounds more professional."*

You might be familiar with or know people who have encountered this scenario: they feel fully engaged in their work, invest considerable effort, strive to show-case their skills, actively contribute in meetings, and aim to meet or exceed expectations. Such individuals appear highly motivated and engaged, right?

Yet, despite their apparent dedication, they may feel demoralized, exhausted, underappreciated, or disconnected from their team behind the scenes. In other words:

They might be highly engaged but highly unhappy employees!

They may appear committed and engaged on the surface, but deep down, they are not experiencing a feeling of contentment and happiness. They have more negative emotions than positive ones despite their high level of engagement in their work, which might lead, in the long term, to a lack of motivation, an increase in burnout, and higher employee turnover.

A study conducted by the Universities of Yale and Leipzig and the School of Management in Düsseldorf[5] showed that nearly 50% of all engaged and highly engaged employees have strong signs of burnout and a high chance of leaving their organizations. These employees are indeed engaged and high achievers, but they are also exhausted and highly stressed.

I am a true believer that employee engagement is vital for a successful workplace, but it must be paired with genuine happiness to sustain long-term success. A lack of happiness can have negative consequences in the long run. When we do not feel good about our work, do not feel like a valued member of the team, or lack trust, our engagement will not be sustainable.

To foster both engagement and happiness, it is necessary to create a safe environment where the team's happiness is embedded in the culture. This approach will indirectly enhance their motivation, performance, and overall engagement.

In summary, while engagement is important, it should go hand in hand with happiness. Both matter!

But despite its significance, happiness is still overlooked as a serious topic. It is often seen as a cliché, and it's not easily addressed in the workplace. Unfortunately, we have so many misconceptions about happiness, particularly at work.

While studying the science of Happiness and Well-being by Dr Laurie R. Santos (American cognitive scientist and professor of psychology at Yale University), I encountered a quote that profoundly shifted my perspective:

Most of the things we think make us happy don't make us as happy as we think.

– Tim Wilson & Dan Gilbert

Isn't it true?

We often tend to believe that a high salary, an impressive job title, cool benefits, or a generous bonus will automatically lead to increased happiness, engagement, and motivation at work.

Professor Santos makes a clear point in her class[6] that once we have a solid foundation, a fair salary, or a good basis, acquiring more of these elements (such as additional income, a job promotion, or enhanced benefits) does not necessarily lead to more happiness, especially in the long term.

When we examine the distinction between individuals who are happy and those who are not, it becomes evident that the key factors are unrelated to financial wealth, job titles, marital status, or material possessions, such as a spacious house or having children.

As Robert J. Waldinger reveals in his eye-opening TED Talk[7] on happiness "What Makes a Good Life? Lessons From the Longest Study on Happiness," our emotional well-being is far more important than our titles or financial gains. Watch his TED Talk via the QR code at the end of this chapter.

The key difference between happy individuals and those who are not lies in attributes such as kindness, social connections, warm relationships, and the feeling of being in a flow state, where they become fully absorbed in their activities and lose track of time.

What can we deduce from this? To maximize your happiness at work, shift your focus from rational factors to emotional fulfillment.

When we speak about happiness at work, it's not just what we **think** about our job but how we **feel** about it that truly matters.

How you feel about your job will have a stronger influence on your engagement and motivation than what you think about it.

In the end:

Happiness is not rational, but rather emotional.

Your Happiness
Your Own Responsibility

I don't know about you, but for a long time, I waited for external factors to improve my happiness before taking action. However, don't you think that your happiness is your own responsibility? Even at work. We cannot wait for our boss or colleagues to make us happier. Of course, they have an influence on us; their emotions and behaviors might impact how we feel, but we are the starting point, and we are in control.

Think about how much time, energy, and money we invest in our personal lives to feel good and have fun. Yet, do we give the same priority to our happiness at work as we do in our personal lives?

It's time to take control of our own happiness. Happiness is an inside job!

Your happiness is your own responsibility.

In my TEDx Talk (check the QR code to watch it), I used a steering wheel on stage to emphasize that we are the drivers of our own happiness. We have the ability to steer our careers and actions in a direction that brings us more fulfillment.

Keep in mind that the goal is not to reach happiness, the goal is to experience it as much as you can!

To achieve this, it is crucial to understand what truly makes you happy at work, what matters to you, and what you need to thrive in the workplace. Define your own version of happiness at work and take the necessary steps to make it a reality.

Now that we've established the importance of happiness at work, let's create your definition of what it means to you.

IDEA 1

FIND YOUR OWN DEFINITION OF HAPPINESS AT WORK

This exercise completely changed my perspective on my own happiness! It all started when my good friend gave me a push and asked me a crucial question: *"What do you need to be happy again at work? You cannot continue to feel frustrated; it's time to take action!"*

It changed my focus. Instead of complaining about feeling frustrated, I began reflecting on what used to make me happy in my job and what would make me happier. The only way I could do that was to discover my definition of happiness at work. It then allowed me to focus my attention on the direction I wanted to go.

By taking ownership of your own happiness, you can create a more fulfilling professional life. We all define happiness differently.

What's your definition of happiness at work?

When I ask this question in teams, I often hear keywords such as recognition, social connection, trust, autonomy, meaningful job, being challenged, clear communication, personal development, and fun.

What would be your keywords?

Now, it's your turn to find your own definition. You can use this self-assessment quiz to help you:

FIND YOUR OWN DEFINITION OF HAPPINESS AT WORK

1. What do you value the most in the workplace?

I value

2. What motivates you at work?

I feel so good and motivated at work when

3. What could you do at the moment to be just a bit happier at work?

I could

3. Think about a specific moment when you were truly happy at work: what did you have, and with whom?

The last time I felt so happy at work was when

Reflect on your previous answers, it will help you identify keywords that contribute to your personal definition of workplace happiness.

List three to five keywords that define happiness at work for you:

1. _____
2. _____
3. _____
4. _____
5. _____

these are your drivers to boost your happiness at work

IDEA 2

5 STEPS TO GET CLOSER TO YOUR DEFINITION OF HAPPINESS

Once you complete the quiz, it will make the following things more transparent to you:

- *What You Have* **=** *Your current situation.*
- *What's Important to You* **=** *Your definition of happiness at work.*

Now, you can get proactive to bridge the gap between your current state and your idea of happiness at work. Remember, happiness isn't a place but a state that fluctuates. What matters is that overall you feel happy at work.

But how?

Here are five steps to implement to get closer to your definition:

1. **You are the starting point**
   First, you need to define:

   - *Which drivers from your definition do you already have in your current situation?*
   - *Which one would you need to do something about it?*

2. **Do something about it**
   Decide what YOU can do (at your level) to get closer to your definition and where you would need support from someone else. Make a clear list and action plan for each of your drivers.

   Here are some examples to inspire you:

   - *To improve [one of your drivers], I'd need to … [complete the sentence]*
   - *Start implementing a routine to …*
   - *Discuss with my partner/colleagues/manager about …*
   - *Schedule a meeting with [whoever] to raise the topic of …*
   - *Brainstorm with my colleague [whoever] on how to improve …*
   - *Ask the opinion of my colleagues about …*
   - *Subscribe to [newsletter/mailing list/magazine, etc.] to improve my skills on …*

The most important thing is to start the conversation with yourself and with those who can help and support you in achieving your definition of happiness at work. Of course, we can't change everything right away; let's be realistic. The purpose isn't to chase happiness, as it's not a destination to be reached but a feeling to be experienced frequently throughout life.

The goal of this exercise is to give you a clear understanding and vision of what makes you happy at work. We often know what exactly frustrates us, yet we tend to overlook what truly drives our happiness.

Let's take my example: I recently did this exercise again, and, by the way, I recommend doing it every year as our definitions can evolve. In my definition, "teamwork" has always been included. Working with people and feeling part of a team has always been very important to me. Since I started my own company, I've realized that the "teamwork" element of my definition of happiness at work has been left unfulfilled. After all, being an entrepreneur comes with wonderful advantages, but it can also be an isolating experience. Until recently, this wasn't really a problem, as my other drivers balanced things out on the positive side. Let's face it: It's hard to get all of your drivers completely fulfilled, and that's okay. However, not being in a team started to bother me more and more. Having a clear understanding of my definition of happiness allows me to focus on it intentionally, helping me take action and steer my efforts in the right direction.

Sure, it's challenging for me to improve this driver overnight, but I've started to become more creative in fostering a sense of teamwork and avoiding loneliness. For example, I've begun collaborating more with other experts and participating in various projects. I've also started developing leadership programs to support leaders in developing their human skills and following them in their leadership journeys for longer periods of time. While these small steps won't replace being part of a team, they will help fulfill the need to be surrounded by people more often.

Take Melissa, a team manager at a Forbes 500 company; one of her drivers was to receive recognition, but it was lacking. Receiving positive feedback and appreciation was a motivator for her to grow and feel empowered, much like most of us. However, it wasn't really part of her team's culture, and she found it hard to ask for recognition. When it's not part of the culture, I always recommend trying to set a new trend by inspiring others. Melissa and I worked together to find creative ways to bring a sense of recognition to the team.

She suggested starting team meetings by celebrating successes and giving more regular positive feedback using fun digital thank-you cards or by using the FBI technique (explained in Chapter 8).

By being proactive and understanding her own definition of happiness, Melissa was able to influence a team culture where recognition, positive feedback, and praise became more common, and people felt valued.

3. Include your colleagues

Ask your close colleagues about their definition of happiness at work. It will promote reflection, understanding, and collaboration among team members.

It could be a nice exercise to do during a team get-together (or even online).

➡ It would allow everyone to reflect and share the main drivers from their definition.

➡ You will understand what matters to them and might understand their way of working much better.

➡ It will encourage everyone to open up and explore how each of you can contribute to getting closer to your main drivers. Supporting each other is crucial to creating a positive work environment.

4. Speak up

Try to have a conversation with your manager to share your definition and your plan to get closer to it. Is there anything your manager could do to support you?

For example, more feedback in meetings, supporting the team on a specific project, more transparency, open communication, etc.

Ensure the discussion does not turn into "blaming" but brings ideas from which you could all benefit. Try to lead the conversation with *"I feel," "I think," "We could," "What do you think of," "Why don't we try..."* etc. Using the feedback techniques in Chapter 8 might be useful for this conversation.

5. **Be inspirational**

   Lead by example and inspire others with your initiatives to get closer to your main definition.

   Happiness is contagious!

   People around you might be inspired by your actions and start imitating your initiatives. It may even be your manager.

Keep in mind:

Happiness is a skill
Happiness is a mindset
Happiness is an attitude

Employees' happiness should no longer be viewed as a non-essential aspect or an exception but as an integral part of corporate strategy. Engagement and productivity are often the results of a happy and motivated workforce rather than the other way around.

We All Play a Role in Shaping Culture

Imagine a company where everyone feels frustrated, lacks enjoyment in their work, finds no meaning in what they do, struggles to get along with colleagues, and shows no respect for one another – coupled with a total absence of positive leadership. Sounds terrible, right? This is an example of what a toxic work culture could look like. And even if you only have a handful of toxic employees within your organization, you'll have other employees who are scared to work with them, and this still impacts team dynamics.

Now, picture a scenario where employees feel good; they know how to boost their positive emotions, have meaning in what they do, experience great teamwork, and demonstrate collaboration, trust, and kindness. Together, everyone can influence such a positive company culture.

Employees shape the culture, and in turn, the culture influences the behaviors of both new and existing employees. Positive cultures tend to encourage positive behaviors, while toxic cultures often perpetuate negative behaviors.

When companies create a positive work environment, they unlock their team's full potential. While it's evident that everyone contributes to a positive environment at work, we need to understand what influences it.

The Factors of a Positive Work Culture

Experts in positive psychology, happiness, and well-being – such as Martin Seligman, Emiliana Simon-Thomas, Tal Ben-Shahar, Sonya Lyubomirsky, and Laurie Santos – emphasize that several factors significantly contribute to a positive work culture. For example, having good working relationships, a sense of purpose and meaning, receiving positive feedback, and experiencing feelings of achievement can strongly lead to increased happiness, engagement, and improved team performance.

Thanks to advancements in positive psychology over the last few decades, we have gained insights into how to influence the above factors.

To build meaningful workplace relationships, it's crucial to nurture a sense of belonging, cultivate positive connections with colleagues and managers, engage in authentic and positive communication, and express gratitude, empathy, and kindness. Incorporating fun experiences at work can indeed further strengthen bonds among employees. Prioritizing these factors undoubtedly enhances trust and relationships in the workplace.

When discussing our feelings of achievement, the emphasis lies not on achievement per se, but rather on cultivating a sense of accomplishment and growth. Receiving recognition and appreciation, learning to give and receive feedback, engaging in meaningful work, and developing our human skills also contribute to our overall development.

There are numerous actions we can take individually or as a team to foster a positive work culture, which we will explore later in this practical guide.

In the upcoming chapters, you will find scientific insights and interviews with inspiring leaders who are making significant contributions in their respective roles. I will explore the various factors throughout the book and share tangible ideas and initiatives implemented by companies of all sizes to inspire you to continue fostering a positive work culture or start doing so if you haven't already.

CHAPTER HIGHLIGHTS

✔

Creating a positive work culture is crucial
in today's fast-paced business world.

✔

Everyone in the organization contributes to the culture.

✔

Employees can be engaged at work <u>and</u> unhappy – the employees'
happiness is important if we want to achieve sustainable team engagement.

✔

Even if external factors might influence it,
you are responsible for your own happiness.

✔

Happiness is not a destination to reach – it's a skill you can train,
a mindset you can master, and an attitude to have.

✔

It's important to know what makes you feel good at work so you can start to
take action and get closer to your own definition of happiness at work.

✔

Having good relationships at work, a sense of progress, a feeling of
achievement, meaning, and purpose will support fostering
a positive work culture.

LET'S TAKE ACTION

➡ Let's measure your happiness level. Rate from 1 to 10:

  ○ *Your happiness in your private life:*

  ○ *Your happiness at work:*

Is there a huge gap between the two, or are they close?

How do you think your level of happiness affects the people around you?

➡ Remember, happiness is a skill – a mindset – an attitude!
  What's the one small thing you can start doing to be "just" a bit happier
  at work?

➡ Write three to five keywords that define your current company culture:

Access additional resources by scanning the QR code.

YOUR THOUGHTS
YOUR JOURNEY

Capture your insights, ideas, and action steps as you make this journey your own.

2

IGNITING POSITIVITY AT WORK

Understand Positive Psychology to Boost Your Positive Emotions at Work

We all experience a combination of emotions at work – both positive and negative. Depending on the day – and the energy we feel coming from the people we work with – one might be more dominant than the other.

Creating a positive work culture doesn't mean we should only feel positive emotions. That would be far from reality.

Faking happiness, ignoring problems, or avoiding negative emotions to appear always positive is not the answer – this can lead to toxic positivity, which we definitely want to avoid.

Of course, it would be great to feel good all the time, but honestly, that's pretty unrealistic.

Experiencing negative or challenging emotions can actually be beneficial. They help us grow, adapt, and make changes. Think about the big changes in your life or the moments of personal growth – often, they come right after a frustrating or negative experience.

It's crucial to avoid falling into a negative cycle; I believe the key is to aim to feel good most of the time. Let's strive for a balance where positive emotions outweigh the negative ones.

Thanks to pioneers like Martin Seligman, an American psychologist and one of the leading researchers in the field, there has been a significant shift since around 2000 towards focusing more on positive emotions.

While traditional psychology often focuses on the negative aspects of people's lives, such as pathology and dysfunction, positive psychology seeks to understand what makes individuals thrive by examining the positive elements of their lives.

Good to know:

Our brain doesn't respond to positivity and negativity in the same way.

Imagine this:

You've had quite a good day at work with engaging meetings. You've even had your favorite lemon pie for dessert with your favorite colleague and ticked off all the urgent tasks on your to-do list. But then, in the afternoon, there comes a negative comment from John, the well-known complainer. Suddenly, all the positive parts of your day seem to fade away. When you come home, what do you end up telling your partner, friend, or family? It's about the negative part of the day – "John's complaining again!" – instead of all the small, good things that happened.

Here is how it works:

We tend to remember negative experiences much more vividly than positive ones.[1] This is known as the brain's negativity bias, a phenomenon well-documented by psychologists.

NEGATIVITY BIAS

Our brains are wired to focus on the negative and overlook the positive.

The science behind negativity bias lies in our brain's evolutionary history. In survival terms, paying extra attention to potential threats or negative situations was crucial for our ancestors. It helped them avoid dangers and stay alive. As a result, our brains develop a bias towards remembering negative experiences much more than positive ones. This bias persists today, influencing how we perceive and recall events.

This is why one negative comment from a colleague feels like a personal attack and can shape the entire day. Honestly, our brains are still stuck in the Stone Age; to them, a grumpy coworker might as well be a lion blocking the office doorway!

Our negativity can be contagious, affecting everyone around us at home and at work – fortunately, so can our positivity!

If you coach yourself, you can hack your brain to see the positive first.

The beauty of focusing on the good is that it forces you to notice the small things we often overlook, like a compliment or a nice conversation with a colleague.

Activating your brain to focus on the good and taking a moment to savor these experiences is where the magic happens! We transform these emotions into positive experiences. This makes the feelings stronger and enduring. That's the power of neuroplasticity – the brain's capacity to continue growing and evolving in response to life experiences.

I learned a lot from Dr. Rick Hanson, a renowned psychologist and author who specializes in the field of positive neuroplasticity. He explores how positive experiences can shape and improve brain structure and function.

In the next expert corner, we dive into the transformative power of positive neuroplasticity, as explained by Dr. Rick Hanson. He offers practical steps for "taking in the good," showing how simple mental practices can rewire the brain for greater resilience and well-being.

With Rick Hanson

The science of positive neuroplasticity shows that every person has the power to change their brain for the better.
— Rick Hanson, PhD

The three basic steps of taking in the good — according to Dr. Rick Hanson, leading expert in positive neuroplasticity:

1. **Have a beneficial experience:** Recognize a feeling you're already experiencing or generate one by reflecting on something that makes you feel thankful.
2. **Enrich it:** Stay with it; allow it to resonate within your body; enjoy it!
3. **Absorb it:** Focus on the feeling of that experience and consciously allow it to become part of you.

The mind can change the brain to change the mind!
— Rick Hanson, PhD

As Dr Rick Hanson explains: In step 1, you activate a mental state, and in steps 2 and 3, you install it in your brain. This works because "neurons that fire together, wire together": mental activity changes neural structure.

Main benefits of taking in the good:

➡ **It builds specific resources inside you**, including the key inner strengths that are matched to your external challenges or internal issues.
➡ **It brings the general benefits of being active** rather than passive, and treating yourself like you matter.
➡ **It sensitizes your brain to the positive**, making it like Velcro for good.
➡ **It creates positive cycles**: By feeling fulfilled yourself, you're more likely to contribute positively to others, which in turn enriches your own experiences and personal development.

Source: Positive Neuroplasticity Training with Rick Hanson in 2021.[2]

By understanding our brain's negativity bias and recognizing our ability to change our thinking and behavior patterns, we can develop new mindsets, memories, skills, and abilities. Now, let's explore practical strategies to counteract this bias and foster positivity in the workplace.

Initiatives to Boost Positive Emotions at Work

In this part, we will delve into science-based practices and simple ideas to apply positive psychology in the work environment, allowing you to find tricks to boost positive emotions in you and those around you.

IDEA 3

REFLECT ON YOUR HIGHLIGHT OF THE DAY

Reflecting on your highlight of the day – or at least your highlight of the week – will help you reduce your negativity bias (as previously explained). Take a moment to recall what made you smile, your small achievements, and the moments that brought you joy.

Make it a daily habit – I personally do it after work and again with my kids before going to bed. It sparks great conversations! Try it during dinner or your evening routine with loved ones.

WHAT'S THE HIGHLIGHT OF YOUR DAY?

EVEN AFTER A CHALLENGING TIME...

...A SMALL HIGHLIGHT CAN BRIGHTEN YOUR DAY!

Also, incorporate this practice with your colleagues:

➡ **Highlight of the week:** During your end-of-week team meetings, make it a tradition to share the highlights of your week. Ask everyone to mention something work-related that made them feel good, something they enjoyed, or are proud of – no matter how small. It has to be specific and recent.

➡ **Use interactive tools** to collect these highlights efficiently. Interactive platforms such as Mentimeter, Slido, or just the chat features in any other communication platform will do! Visualizing and discussing them can be quick; even a few minutes will have a great impact. I've done it with an audience of a few hundred during my online sessions.

➡ **Highlight wall:** Set up a wall near the coffee machine/printer or any strategic space in the office where employees can write their weekly highlights. It's a simple way to foster positivity and connection. For remote or hybrid teams, create a digital wall or a chat dedicated to the highlights on your team's communication channel.

IDEA 4

10 IMPACTFUL QUESTIONS TO REFLECT ON YOUR WORKDAY

Reflecting, journaling, or discussing these impactful questions will help you review the reality of your day. Sometimes, we are caught in our own hamster wheel and don't even realize that we actually had a good day or that we successfully completed a task that was causing us stress.

- *What went well today?*
- *What did I learn or find interesting?*
- *Who did I help/support?*
- *What did I achieve?*
- *Where did I use my strengths?*

- *What positive impacts did I have today?*
- *How did I manage my challenges/negative emotions?*
- *Is there anything I could have done differently?*
- *Did I have more positive or negative experiences?*
- *Who/What made me smile today?*

These questions will hopefully help you zoom in. Of course, you don't need to answer all of them at once, but consider picking one or two per day and being as specific as possible in your answers. This might also help you visualize how you want tomorrow to be after such a day!

Feel free to adapt these questions during your next 1:1 with a team member!

IDEA 5

THE 21-DAY POSITIVITY CHALLENGE

Research and many experts have shown that gratitude, kindness, and praise are powerful tools for boosting positivity at work and fostering a positive work culture.

To help you harness these benefits, I've created a 21-day positivity challenge for both you and your colleagues. While some experts suggest that it takes about 21 days to change habits, I believe that the time it really takes can vary from person to person. Let's use the 21-day guideline as inspiration rather than a strict rule.

This challenge is designed to help you establish routines and train your brain to focus more on the positive aspects of your work life. Twenty-one days might do the work, but extend it until it becomes more natural to you.

Feel free to draw inspiration from this challenge, adapt it to your own situation, or download it via the QR code at the end of this chapter to share with your team.

21-DAY

POSITIVITY CHALLENGE

TO BOOST GRATITUDE, RECOGNITION, PRAISE & FUN

DAY 1
Celebrate your own wins

DAY 2
Share the highlight of the week with your team

DAY 3
Thank someone who helped you lately

DAY 4
Start a meeting with positivity

DAY 5
If you need to apologize to someone, it's time to do it!

DAY 6
Reflect on what you are grateful for

DAY 7
No complaining day

DAY 8
Ask for feedback on how you can improve something

DAY 9
Say a 'real' thank you

DAY 10
Take a walk outside with a colleague you appreciate

DAY 11
Celebrate the team's big & small successes

DAY 12
Compliment someone – and be honest!

DAY 13
Praise someone for her/his good work

DAY 14
Serve a cup of coffee/tea or a favorite drink to a busy colleague

DAY 15
Give positive feedback

DAY 16
Reflect on what you are looking forward to this week

DAY 17
Today help at least one colleague

DAY 18
Smile more at the people around you

DAY 19
Show empathy

DAY 20
Write nice notes to leave on your colleagues' desks or send via sms

DAY 21
Send one of your happy songs to a colleague who needs a boost of energy

As the expert, Jim Kwik (American Brain Coach and NYT Bestselling Author) explains in one of his videos: Gratitude is a superpower to boost positivity for ourselves and around us. When you experience gratitude, your brain releases neurotransmitters (like dopamine and serotonin) that help you feel good and regulate your mood. Over time, practicing gratitude rewires your brain, creating new patterns that help you boost resilience, reduce stress, and stay focused and positive.

Implementing this challenge will give you ideas on practices you can easily turn into a habit that sustains you all year long.

IDEA 6

THE BRAVO WALL

During my workshop at the multinational pharmaceutical company Sanofi, the team I worked with used their official online recognition program, called Bravo, to create a "Bravo Wall" directly in the meeting room during their annual in-person workshop.

Many companies have employee recognition systems in place. The aim of these platforms is to acknowledge employees' efforts, provide recognition and praise, and reward them for their contributions in the workplace. Even if your company does not have an official recognition system in place, you can easily create a "Bravo Wall" in the office or at your next team meeting.

The purpose of such a wall is to share positive feedback, praise, or recognition with your colleagues.

Steps to create a Bravo Wall:

➡ Get medium-sized envelopes.
➡ Write the name of your colleague on each envelope or attach a picture of them (you can take fun pictures at the beginning of the workshop with an instant camera). Use one envelope per person.
➡ Stick each envelope on a wall, window, or whiteboard.

- Provide sticky notes or nice cards for colleagues to write down kind words, positive feedback, or praise about their colleagues.
- Ask participants to put their messages in the appropriate envelope.
- At the end of the session, everyone can take their envelopes and read their messages.

You can call it a Bravo Wall, Appreciation Wall, Feedback Wall, Wall of Praise, Recognition Wall, or Cheers Your Peers. Be creative and adapt it to your meeting format. You can easily create an online version using interactive platforms. Check the QR code to get some inspiration.

It's a nice way to boost morale, give recognition, and encourage positive feedback.

IDEA 7

THE APPRECIATION FOLDER

One of my clients came up with an original idea by creating an "appreciation folder" on his computer where he collects all the positive feedback, small achievements, big successes, or nice emails he receives from his team members, managers, or clients. He explained to me once that whenever he feels a bit low, loses his sense of purpose, or has doubts, he looks at his appreciation folder to give himself a boost of joy and a sense of pride.

I think this is an excellent idea that can inspire you to create something similar. You can adapt it to your own style and situation, whether it's a folder on your computer, a wall, or a happy email folder.

Give it a fun name and add some spark to it! "My Kudos Kit/Happy Folder/Bravo Box."

Remember, it's essential to take time to appreciate the good things and small wins, and this appreciation folder can help you focus on and remember the positives during challenging times.

IDEA 8

HAPPICARDS: A FUN KUDOS FOR A BIG IMPACT

According to the Oxford dictionary, a kudos is a praise and honor received for an achievement.

When we know how important appreciation is for boosting team morale, creativity, and productivity, we understand its effectiveness in uplifting the people we work with!

Unlike the formal shout-outs during conference calls or feedback forms some large organizations use, I wanted this to have a fun and happy vibe! That's why I created my own Happicards: kudos cards supercharged with playfulness and laughter!

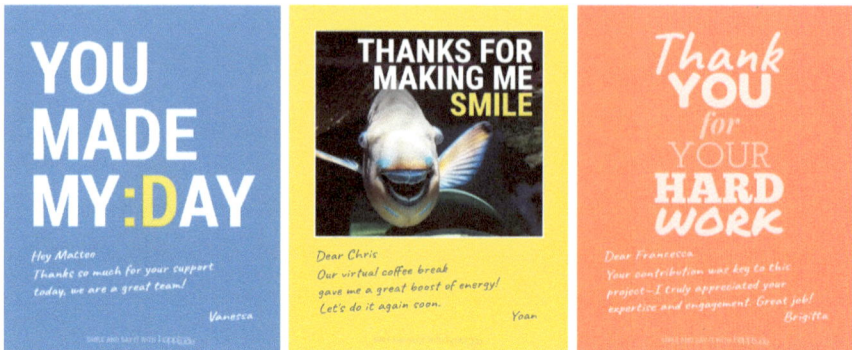

Scan the QR code for access to my free virtual Happicards. Choose your free Happicard – add your personalized message – and send your kudos to someone to spark more positivity!

Let me explain the importance of recognition and praise:

Did you know that when we perform an act of kindness, our brain's reward system gets activated? So, basically, doing something nice for someone else gives us a happiness boost too! It's the tiniest things that make the biggest impact.

To stay motivated, we also need to feel like our voice matters, that we can trust our managers and that our contribution is recognized. The thing about sharing appreciation is that it doesn't have to be a big gesture, new title, or $$ bonus. It's about expressing thanks and showing that we noticed the hard work, creativity, or participation.

Let's not forget that we are primates with a brain that hasn't changed much over hundreds of thousands of years. We feel boosted by positive feedback!

It's so simple to do that no manager can use a "no-budget" excuse.

True recognition has a transformative effect on people. It creates a culture of trust where colleagues bond and become teammates. Because we become a team, we share a purpose and work together towards a common goal. That's why employee recognition is so powerful.

Employee recognition doesn't have to go top to bottom. You can easily share your recognition with people across your organization, from your managers to your peers! And with my free Happicards, you can make it fun!

IDEA 9

THE PONCHO EXERCISE

This is a fun and engaging exercise that works well with colleagues who know each other or at the end of a full-day workshop or project.

The goal is to write something nice or kind about the other person and share positive feedback. It's quite similar to the "Bravo Wall" explained earlier, but here, it's a different format, and the content is not necessarily focused on recognition.

Here's how to do it:

➡ Use a sheet of large flipchart paper per person.
➡ Make a hole in the middle so every participant can pass it over their head.

- Give one flipchart pen per participant.
- Ask each participant to write a kind note, positive message, or some praise on the back of every other person's poncho.
- Give enough time to the participants (10–20 minutes, depending on the group size).
- Once everyone is done, give them extra time to review their messages and the ones from others.

The best time to do it is usually at the end of a full-day meeting, conference, or workshop or before a coffee break or networking session.

You can adapt your support in the following ways:

- You can provide large white T-shirts with special pens, which is the best way to make sure everyone remains with a nice souvenir.
- Or you can do it completely online using interactive tools such as Padlet, Miro, etc.

IDEA 10

NO COMPLAINING DAY

Let's be honest, it can feel satisfying to complain – at least from time to time. I know it does for me!

Complaining is often easier than addressing the problem directly. While it allows us to vent, it also leads to several negative outcomes: it wastes time, affects relationships, creates disengagement, amplifies frustrations, erodes trust, and can make the complainer appear pessimistic.

Did you know? The average person complains between 15 and 30 times a day, according to Will Bowen, the author of *The Complaint-Free World*.[3]

This number is quite shocking! Now, do you want the reputation of the "popular complainer"? Nobody does.

So, how can we reduce complaining?

The first step is recognizing when you complain excessively or fall into patterns of negative thinking. Then, consciously notice when you start to complain about something that doesn't need to be complained about and choose to respond differently – perhaps by practicing gratitude, reframing your thoughts, or fostering optimism. Remember that we have a negativity bias, and we actively need to hack our brains to remember the positive experiences instead of always focusing on the negative.

Starting with a "no complaining day" can be an effective and fun way to become aware of how often you might feel inclined to complain.

I have seen teams implement "no complaining week" – it can be lots of fun and mind-blowing to see how many times we usually complain. You can add a fun twist to stick to it: Use reminder notes, announce it loud and clear in the office, and set up a fun penalty for complaining (like a jar where people add coins for each complaint).

Give it a try; you'll be surprised by the results! Check Chapter 8 on feedback to learn how to handle complainers.

Positive Communication = Improved Workplace Dynamics

In today's workplace, effective communication is fundamental to the success of every team. Maintaining a positive approach to communication is crucial for promoting a healthy work culture. When we speak with encouragement and empathy, it does wonders: it boosts morale, builds trust, and strengthens relationships. This makes everyone feel valued and ready to work together, which not only lifts individual performance but also drives our team to succeed.

Here are a few tips on how to inject more positivity into team conversations:

IDEA 11

THE POWER OF WORDS – MIND YOUR LANGUAGE!

Though it may feel like our thoughts run wild beyond our control, we actually have the power to guide them toward positivity or negativity. What remains beyond our control, however, is the profound effect our negative self-talk can have on our well-being and on those around us.

**Words are powerful,
including those we whisper to ourselves.**

Negative self-talk like *"I'm stupid"* or *"I can't do it"* can lead us to internalize these ideas, impacting our self-esteem, mood, and actions. This self-sabotage is dangerous because we start to embody the very criticisms we level against ourselves. Yet, the reverse is also true! Choosing our internal dialogue carefully and treating ourselves with kindness can transform our outlook.

We tend to experience more of what we focus on, so it's important to practice kindness towards ourselves and nurture our self-worth. Instead of criticizing yourself, try offering words of encouragement and love.

For example, adding the word "yet" at the end of a sentence, such as *"I can't do this ... yet"* or *"I don't know how to do that ... yet"* can help you build self-confidence and cultivate a growth mindset.

What about the words we use at work?

The way we talk to others and the words we choose can either foster a team-oriented environment filled with gratitude, inspiration, and appreciation or promote individualism, frustration, conflict, and even mobbing to some extent.

Great leaders and colleagues utilize the power of positive communication to cultivate an atmosphere of trust, inclusion, respect, and teamwork.

For example, consider using "we" instead of "I" or "our" instead of "my" when speaking to the team (_"We did this / we can do it / our clients / our decisions,"_ etc.)

Your vocabulary at work can either build positivity or negativity, inclusion or exclusion, strengths or weaknesses.

Five powerful words or sentences to use more in the workplace:

- *Thank you.* – Expressing a genuine thank you can boost morale and strengthen team bonds – such simple words but still not used enough or properly.

- *Your contribution was key in this project.* – Recognizing someone's effort and accomplishments fosters a culture of appreciation and gratitude.

- *I believe in you.* – Demonstrating trust in a colleague's skills can boost their confidence and drive.

- *How can we help?* – Offering support not only eases stress but also promotes a collaborative environment.

- *Great job on that project!* – Specific praise can reinforce positive behavior and long-term success.

IDEA
12
INSPIRATIONAL FRIDAY

Friday (or the last day of your working week) is a great way to reflect on the week and plan the week ahead. Since I started taking a moment every Friday to reflect on the past week and plan what's waiting for me in the next one, my weekends and Monday mornings have completely changed.

The purpose of organizing an Inspirational Friday is to inspire the employees to finish the week on a positive note and have a moment to pause and reflect. This can be done by spreading inspirational quotes, powerful or fun messages, self-reflection exercises, articles, or team-action ideas.

Here are some tips for creating an "Inspirational Friday":

➡️ Use one of the company's communication channels to spread the message (it can be weekly email, messages on Slack, WhatsApp, Teams, screens in the office, internal social media, etc.).

➡️ Be inspired by this book's content to create quotes, messages, or activities. For example, the positivity challenge, explained earlier, or the five icebreakers and conversation starters explained in Chapter 5 could be used for this.

➡️ Inspire the team to share their answers on the communication channels or to pause and take a moment to reflect.

➡️ Create a mix of action, self-reflection messages, fun messages, and team challenges. Avoid asking the same question or sharing the same content every Friday.

You can turn Inspirational Friday into a communication campaign for a few weeks to reinforce positivity at work and share ideas on how to foster a positive work culture. I've designed many communication campaigns for my clients, and usually, employees like to learn and engage in the posts.

IDEA 13

5 WAYS TO ADD HAPPINESS TO YOUR BUSINESS EMAILS

We all have our own style of writing and sending business emails.

It can be super formal, straightforward, too direct – or too friendly.

Sometimes, we don't even realize how the people on the other side perceive us. Reading our emails, they might think we're aggressive, mean, or bossy. And then, when they meet us and have a real conversation, they say, *"Hey, you're nothing like how you sound in your emails!"*

So, what's the solution to ensure you don't sound too negative in your emails, even when delivering difficult messages? Adding a bit of happiness to your business emails might be a good way. Here are five things to try (and maybe not all at once!):

1. **Add a pleasant and personalized greeting**
   - *Hey, [Name], Happy Monday!/Happy Friday!*
   - *I hope you're having a positive week!*
   - *I'm eager to get your advice on [subject].*
   - *How did [recent project] turn out?*
   - *I loved your recent [photo/article/social media post].*

2. **Add a sense of humor (if it's appropriate)**
   - *I hope you've had your coffee already!*
   - *Hello from the other side.*
   - *Hi, it's me again, but don't worry – I'll keep it short!*
   - *Hello, my favorite colleague.*

3. **Use emojis to express your emotions (= digital body language)**
   Depending on the context, emojis can be an effective way for us to express our emotions and body language digitally. I usually use emojis to reinforce positivity, to celebrate successes, or when I am sharing a challenge or have a request. These are my favorites emojis for business communications:
   😊 👍 🙌 👏 🤩 🤯 ⚙️ 🙂 🙏
   It goes without saying that we shouldn't add emojis at the end of every sentence in all our emails! Instead, let's choose the right moment (not to mention the right audience!) to express our emotions and body language with emojis. A single emoji might be all you need.

4. **Add encouragement/recognition/positivity**
   Receiving positive feedback/recognition/praise from others helps us feel seen and gives us a sense of having achieved something. It motivates us to keep working to a high standard. It's a form of positive reinforcement.

   Positive sentences in an email can change its tone and influence how the receiver responds.

   Here are a few examples you can use, depending on the context:
   - *I really appreciated your help on this project.*
   - *Your support is making such a difference.*
   - *We are such a great team, I love working with all of you!*

- *I realize how complex the project is, I really appreciate your hard work.*
- *I really valued your insights during the meeting today – thanks for raising that point.*
- *Sending you positive vibes for your presentation today.*

5. Finish on a positive note

The way you wrap up your email is super important. It's like saying goodbye when you meet someone face-to-face. Remember to end your message politely or add kind words where appropriate.

You could try writing:

- *Wishing you a happy day!*
- *I hope you have a positive and productive afternoon!*
- *Enjoy your lunch break!*
- *I wish you a successful day.*
- *Wishing you a well-deserved rest this weekend!*
- *Let's catch up again soon – it would be great to see you!*
- *I wish you a lovely day – breathe and smile.*

No matter what your email is about (even if you're sharing something challenging, asking someone to do something, setting a new task, etc.), it shouldn't stop you from adding kindness and positivity. Of course, you must consider your audience and choose what's appropriate for the receiver. Obviously, you wouldn't send the same things to new clients or top management as you would to, say, a close colleague.

And remember:

It's not about making the email twice as long and sending fake positivity.

The goal is not to apply everything all at once. My best tip is to keep it simple and mean what you say for maximum results. Less is sometimes more!

IDEA 14

ADD A POSITIVE TWIST TO YOUR OUT-OF-OFFICE

Vacations or time off are meant for relaxation, exploration, and unwinding, so why should your out-of-office message be boring? Incorporating well-placed humor into your automated replies can bring a smile to your colleagues' faces and reflect your fun-loving personality. An effective out-of-office message should be informative, manage expectations, offer support or a solution, and add a fun twist while maintaining professionalism. It should, of course, align with the communication style of your workplace.

Here are four ideas to inspire your next out-of-office reply:

1. **Start with a captivating greeting**
   Set the tone right from the beginning with a catchy and amusing greeting:

   - *Greetings from the wilderness!*

   - *Good day to you from the middle of nowhere*

   - or a simple *Hello* in the language of where you are, like *Bonjour* or *Hola*

2. **Inject humor into your return date**
   Instead of simply stating when you'll be back, have some fun with it.

   - *I'll be back on [return date] and ready to dive back into work.*

3. **Include a fun fact or travel-inspired joke**
   Enhance your out-of-office message by sharing a fun fact or incorporating a joke related to your vacation spot or travel in general. This adds an extra layer of amusement.

4. **Offer alternative sources of help**
   While your out-of-office message may be humorous, it's essential to provide assistance options for urgent matters. Direct your colleagues to alternative contacts or resources that can help them during your absence. You can combine helpfulness with humor, such as:

   - *If you need immediate assistance, please reach out to my incredible colleague, Sarah. She's a superhero!*

Writing a funny out-of-office message not only lightens the mood but also showcases your creativity and leaves a positive impression on your colleagues.

Remember to strike a balance between humor and professionalism, ensuring that the message conveys your unavailability while providing useful information—no need to add a joke in every sentence.

This chapter has outlined various strategies to enhance positivity at work, both individually and within teams. Remember that not all initiatives need to be implemented at once; select the ones that resonate most with you and give them a try. As you strive to create a positive atmosphere, it's essential to prioritize authenticity and genuineness – positivity has a greater impact when it comes from a real place. When we approach each day with a sincere commitment to fostering a supportive environment, our actions naturally inspire trust, deepen connections, and lead to lasting change. Small, consistent efforts, when paired with authenticity, can transform not only our workspaces but also the people around us.

Bringing more positivity to surround your life will significantly impact your overall well-being. In the next chapter, we'll explore how prioritizing employee well-being can be a core cultural pillar in organizations.

CHAPTER HIGHLIGHTS

✓

Creating a positive work culture isn't about feeling positive emotions all the time. Instead, aim to cultivate an environment where positive emotions outweigh the negative ones.

✓

Our brains are naturally wired to focus on the negative due to a natural negativity bias. That's why we tend to remember bad experiences more vividly than good ones.

✓

We can reprogram our minds to focus on the positives by reflecting on daily highlights, practicing gratitude, and fostering recognition and kindness in our interactions.

✓

By acknowledging difficult emotions instead of suppressing them, we can move through them with greater ease and less intensity.

✓

Words matter! Positive communication not only boosts morale and productivity but also strengthens relationships and builds trust within the team.

LET'S TAKE ACTION

➡️ Ask your colleagues or someone you see tomorrow about their highlight of the week.

➡️ Try to implement one initiative for yourself and one for your team to boost positive emotions at work.

➡️ How can you adapt your communication style to spread more positivity around you?

Access additional resources by scanning the QR code.

YOUR THOUGHTS
YOUR JOURNEY

Capture your insights, ideas, and action steps as you make this journey your own.

3

MAKING WELL-BEING A CORE CULTURAL PILLAR

Workplaces Can Drive Mental Health and Well-Being

Experts have long known that having a positive mental state can lead to better physical health, growth, and longer lifespan. This means that taking care of your mind can greatly benefit your entire body.

While many challenges outside the workplace can influence our mental health and well-being, work plays a crucial role in our lives and significantly impacts it as well. When people feel fulfilled in their jobs, they are more likely to experience positive physical and mental health and make constructive contributions to their workplace. On the other hand, a work environment with high stress, poor communication, lack of support, and unfair practices can negatively impact employees' mental health, leading to issues such as stress, burnout, and depression.

The COVID-19 pandemic emphasized the importance of organizations supporting their employees' mental health and well-being to maintain a productive and healthy workforce.

Many organizations are investing more money and resources to prioritize the health and well-being of their employees as an integral aspect of their overall business approach.

It is becoming clear that employees now expect companies to prioritize their well-being actively.

Research shows that employees are more likely to choose employers who invest in creating a supportive work environment.[1] Prioritizing employee well-being is no longer just a perk; it is a strategic necessity for attracting and retaining the best talent.

Well-being refers to being healthy, happy, and wealthy in different aspects of life. It includes having good mental health, high life satisfaction, a sense of meaning or purpose, personal growth, and the ability to manage stress. In a professional environment, we often refer to these different dimensions of well-being: mental, physical, emotional, social, financial, and holistic well-being.

Some workplaces may prioritize mental health in response to the significant impact of work-related stress on productivity and health costs. Others may take a broader approach, considering overall employee well-being to encompass a wide range of factors influencing satisfaction and effectiveness.

This chapter features various studies demonstrating the positive impact of implementing a holistic well-being strategy, which can help you convince the top management to take a more active role in employee well-being. Be sure to check the next "Fact Corner" section for key insights and compelling data to support your case.

We will look at examples of strategies you can implement or use as inspiration, as well as initiatives aimed at improving both your own well-being and that of your team members. You will also find case studies from companies and cover initiatives that can be implemented on an individual, team, and/or cultural level.

➡ **Companies with higher employee well-being scores outperform their counterparts in multiple traditional measures of firm performance[2]**
These companies demonstrate increased firm value, higher return on assets, and elevated profits compared to their counterparts with lower well-being scores.

➡ **Leadership style impacts employees' mental health[3]**
Leaders who cultivate a vision, consider people's needs, and invest in positive relationships report better mental health outcomes in their teams. Conversely, employees with destructive leaders experience worse mental health.

➡ **"Good health and well-being" has been an established goal of the United Nations' sustainable development goals since their introduction[4]**
From 2024, under the EU Corporate Sustainability Reporting Directive (CSRD), large companies are required to disclose environmental, social, and governance (ESG) metrics, including detailed reports on their sustainability practices, showing specifically the risks and opportunities related to these goals.

➡ **60% of employees, 64% of managers, and 75% of the c-suite are seriously considering quitting for a job that would better support their well-being[5]**
This highlights the growing demand for healthier work environments where people feel valued, supported, and balanced. Many employees report experiencing frequent stress and exhaustion, driving them to seek workplaces that prioritize their well-being.

Craft Your Company's Well-Being Strategy

There are many ways to craft a well-being strategy. In this section, you will find some examples of how to craft one for your company, and we will discuss some ideas and initiatives you can implement to improve your own well-being and mental health, as well as that of those around you.

First of all, evaluating what's already in place and reflecting on the following factors is essential.

IDEA 15

10 QUESTIONS TO REFLECT ON BEFORE CRAFTING YOUR STRATEGY

Before developing any kind of well-being strategy, brainstorm the following questions with the team responsible:

- *How is well-being integrated into your organizational culture?*
- *What are the specific well-being and mental health needs within your organization?*
- *What policies and initiatives do you already have in place?*
- *How do employees engage with the available initiatives?*
- *What gets in the way of well-being in your organization?*
- *Which KPIs are already established related to your employees' health and well-being?*
- *What do you want to achieve/what's your main goal in terms of well-being and mental health?*
- *What level of commitment does leadership show towards mental health and well-being?*
- *How will you measure the success of the initiatives?*
- *What will be in place, and who will be responsible for developing and implementing the initiatives?*

Once you respond to these questions, you will have a better understanding of where your company or team stands. It's not always necessary to create a new strategy or implement something from scratch. This step might help you realize what you need to adapt instead of creating something completely new.

It's becoming more common for companies to have dedicated teams in charge of taking care of their employees' well-being and mental health. It's often integrated within the Diversity, Equity, and Inclusion (DEI) or Culture departments. Some even create positions such as Chief Well-Being Officer, Corporate Health Manager, or Head of Global Well-being.

On the other hand, some companies prefer to establish task forces, focus groups, or well-being champions, which are groups of employees involved in these matters. Later in this chapter, we will look at an example from the company Sonova on how they engaged worldwide well-being champions in their company.

**Regardless of the approach,
it's important to have a well-being strategy
that matches your company's needs and goals.**

Having a proper structure in place will help ensure your employees' well-being is taken care of and help track its impact.

Here are two different ways to implement a well-being strategy:

- ➡ Take inspiration or craft your strategy using the renowned U.S. Surgeon General's Framework.
- ➡ Develop your own comprehensive strategy based on the four steps I will outline later.

Tailor the strategy or framework that makes the most sense with your company's current needs and objectives.

IDEA 16
GET INSPIRED BY THE U.S. SURGEON GENERAL'S FRAMEWORK

If you're starting from scratch and have no well-being strategy in place, the U.S. Surgeon General's Framework for Workplace Mental Health & Well-Being will help you understand the foundation that workplaces can build upon. It outlines the foundational role that workplaces should play in promoting the health and well-being of workers. You will find their complete guide by scanning the QR code.

As they explain:

> The Surgeon General's Framework for Workplace Mental Health & Well-Being is intended to **spark organizational dialogue and change in the workplace**. Centered around the foundational principles of equity and the voices of all workers, it includes **five essentials** and necessary components for addressing workplace mental health and well-being based on human needs.
>
> This Framework contributes to decades of public health, economic, sociological, and organizational psychology research. Organizations can use this Framework to support their workplaces as engines of mental health and well-being.
>
> - U.S. Surgeon General's Framework for Workplace Mental Health & Well-Being

You can follow this framework and analyze each essential pillar to develop initiatives within your company – check the QR code for more information.

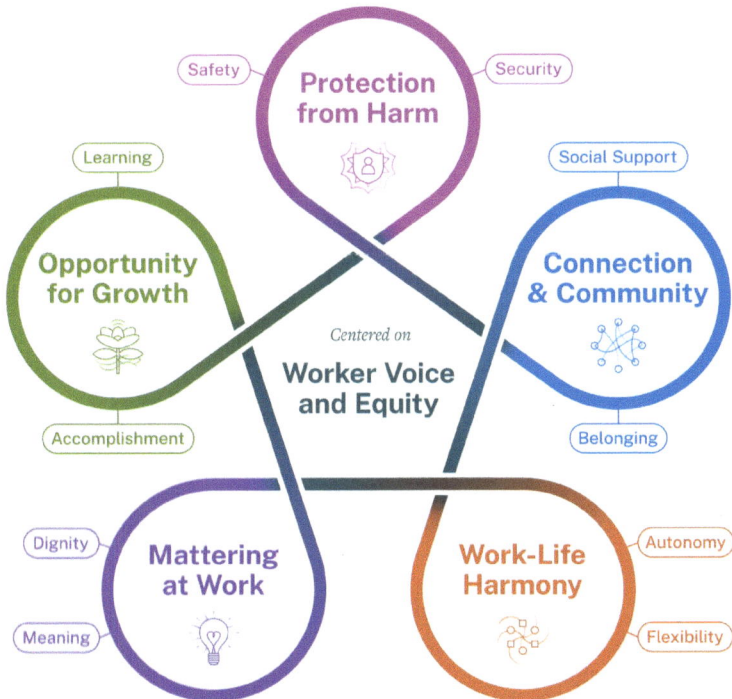

Source: The 5 Essentials for Workplace Mental Health and Well-Being. U.S. Surgeon General's Framework for Workplace Mental Health & Well-Being.[6]

IDEA
17

I believe that the most effective strategy aligns with your company's culture, industry, KPIs, and workforce. It's important to consider these factors when deciding on a plan of action.

Having a more general strategy than following the detailed framework previously explained might be more beneficial for some companies, depending on your objectives.

I often use the following four steps to develop a strategy for fostering a positive work culture: awareness, analysis, taking action, and follow-up.

You can either create your strategy from scratch or adapt an existing one with these four steps.

1. **Raise awareness**

   Raising awareness about the importance of mental health and well-being is crucial for initiating positive change. To ensure employees are actively involved and engaged with new initiatives, they must first understand the importance of implementing a well-being strategy. We also need to empower employees to recognize the signs of poor mental health and well-being to be able to seek and offer support before reaching a crisis point. Spreading the word is a crucial step.

   Here are two initiatives I like to implement to increase awareness within teams:

   → Facilitate awareness and informative sessions (such as webinars, workshops, trainings, lunch and learns, and inspirational talks) to open the conversation, create prevention, and teach employees topics such as mental and physical well-being, mental health, happiness at work, psychological safety, burnout, stress management, EQ, etc.

   → Inform and spread knowledge through different channels (newsletter, internal platforms, tools, etc.). It can be inspirational nuggets, science-based evidence, insightful articles, or reminders for initiatives.

2. **Analyze well-being on an individual and team level**

This step could be done before, at the same time, or after the awareness part. It might depend on what is already in place in your company and how you want to craft your strategy. It's a crucial step to gather data, evaluate it, and implement solutions.

- Measure the employees' well-being (I'll develop this point in more detail in the next section).
- Educate leaders and employees to recognize, identify, and evaluate mental health symptoms.
- Identify skills and knowledge gaps.
- Analyze your desired workplace well-being vision for the company.

3. **Take action**

- Co-creation in Focus Groups, Ambassadors, Champions, or Train the Trainers program to follow up and support well-being initiatives.
- Create a well-being roadmap and implement initiatives step by step.
- Give employees the right tools and training for their skills development.
- Build relationships and increase the sense of belonging.
- Refer to the U.S. Surgeon Framework to select which of the five essentials needs to be improved.

4. **Follow up for sustainable results**

- Continue to spread awareness and ensure high engagement in well-being initiatives.
- Track and analyze the success of initiatives.
- Leadership ownership: involve leaders to be active, lead, and follow up on initiatives.
- Focus groups, Ambassadors, or Champions need to be active and engaging.
- Your company's well-being strategy needs to evolve and adapt to the current situation, new goals, and the company's culture.

Whether to use the U.S. Surgeon General's Framework as a guideline or adapt your own strategy is entirely your choice. It's not always necessary to start from scratch to make a change. Companies can build on existing initiatives. Often, it comes down to priorities and a shift in mindset.

A common issue often seen is the gap between intention and execution; a company may have numerous well-being initiatives in place, but employees may not engage with them. This can happen if employees feel overwhelmed by the requirements or believe they are not permitted to implement changes at work. To achieve sustainable results, we must address the root causes of a lack of well-being rather than just applying quick fixes to the symptoms. Teaching, empowering, and guiding employees toward meaningful behavioral change is crucial for long-term success.

Measure Your Workplace Well-Being

Elaborating a well-being strategy is a great step, but keep in mind that you need to measure the employees' well-being levels and the results of your strategy. Make sure you add relevant and measurable elements for each step of your strategy. In this section, you will find a list of questions to ask employees and different measures to pay attention to, giving you a good sense of your analysis.

IDEA 18

ASK THE RIGHT QUESTIONS IN YOUR WELL-BEING SURVEYS

According to the University of Oxford Well-Being Research Centre[7], asking the following four questions will help you measure and track workplace subjective well-being:

On a scale from 0 (not at all) to 10 (completely):

- ○ *Overall, how satisfied are you with your job?*
- ○ *How happy did you feel while at work during the past week?*
- ○ *How stressed did you feel while at work during the past week?*

○ *Overall, how purposeful and meaningful do you find your work?*

The answers to these questions will provide a good indication of employees' well-being based on their job satisfaction, happiness, stress level, and purpose. However, we can take it a step further and ask additional questions related to: sense of achievement, sense of belonging, energy level, flexibility, personal growth, management, appreciation, trust, and support. The following questions will support you to measure those:

○ *How often do you feel that your achievements at work are recognized and valued by your team and supervisors?*

○ *Do you believe there are adequate opportunities for professional growth and development in our organization?*

○ *How effectively does your manager communicate with you about any concerns you might have?*

○ *How would you describe your relationship with other members of your team?*

○ *If you could change one thing about your workplace to improve your well-being, what would it be, and how would it positively impact you in the workplace?*

IDEA 19

10 WELL-BEING QUESTIONS FOR LEADERS TO ASK EMPLOYEES

Sending surveys regularly to assess employees' well-being can be beneficial if it's well done. However, we shouldn't stop there. Team meetings, 1:1 catch-ups, or walk and talks can be great and less formal formats to ask relevant and straightforward questions and gain insight into your team's overall well-being. This can enable you to regularly identify when additional support may be needed.

Here are ten questions you can ask your team to evaluate and support their well-being (no need to ask all of them every week; you can use some of these questions in your meetings, 1:1 informal discussions, or team surveys).

○ *What does "well-being" mean to you?*

- *How would you rate your current mental/physical well-being?*
- *What can you do this week to take care of your well-being?*
- *What gives you energy, and what drains your energy at work?*
- *Do you feel you're getting enough rest to feel refreshed and energized?*
- *What's one thing that supports your well-being and is non-negotiable to you?*
- *How often do you start the day feeling refreshed and full of energy?*
- *How satisfied are you with the relationships you have with your colleagues/leaders?*
- *On a scale of 1–10, how happy are you at work?*
- *How can I support you better so that you can take care of your well-being?*

Asking these questions regularly will not only help evaluate the team's well-being but also raise awareness, allowing each employee to reflect on their own well-being and take action to improve it.

IDEA 20

OTHER MEASUREMENTS OF EMPLOYEES' WELL-BEING

It's important to remember that in order to measure our team's well-being, happiness, or engagement, we should not only focus on quantitative facts but also qualitative ones. There are numerous situations you can start paying attention to and tracking to get a good sense of your employees' well-being. The goal is not to over-measure but to measure what matters for your company's culture (sometimes less is more!).

Here is a list of measurement examples you can take into consideration (both on a quantitative and qualitative level) to assess employees' mental health, engagement and/or holistic well-being:

→ Surveys and self-assessments on mental health and on the different dimensions of well-being

→ Number of sick days and absenteeism

→ Evaluation in 1:1 meetings to discuss personal challenges and goals

- Monitoring mental health through interviews/discussions with employees
- Engagement rate in meetings (are people showing up? Are they willing to speak up, bring ideas, and interact?)
- Engagement rate in company learning mental health/well-being platform (e.g., number of clicks, downloads, engagement in the platform)
- Employee interactions in teams (based on their questions, support, trust, and collaboration)
- Work relationships and dynamics of teams (based on their sense of belonging, getting together, having fun, creativity level)
- Number of participants in well-being initiatives

Measure what makes sense for your well-being strategy.

You will find more examples later in this chapter of how the company Sonova measures and tracks the impact of its mental health and well-being initiatives.

Develop
Well-Being Initiatives

Once you have your strategy planned, it's time to start implementing different well-being initiatives. Let's not focus only on the individual level – we also need an organizational change.

Research shows that taking only an individual approach will be less beneficial than adopting organizational-level approaches as the foundation for good holistic well-being, followed by individual approaches[8].

In a recent Deloitte survey, 80% of employees reported struggling with heavy workloads and stressful jobs. Leaders should prioritize changing job conditions to reduce employee stress and create opportunities for integrating personal development into the workday, rather than focusing solely on how employees manage stress through practices that require extra effort to see benefits.[9]

There are many possible initiatives to promote workplace well-being. Depending on the dimensions you would like to focus on, other chapters (e.g., Chapter 9 on stress management) might also be helpful for holistic well-being. In this particular chapter, I have selected a few well-being initiatives that you can implement at work for yourself, your team, and the whole company. Additionally, you will find case studies with real examples from multinational companies, providing a realistic approach to implementing global well-being initiatives.

IDEA
21

CHARGE
YOUR BATTERY

It's important for individuals to be aware of what energizes and drains them daily. By understanding this, individuals can take action to improve practices to regain energy, take care of themselves, and maintain their overall well-being.

Having your battery fully or well charged puts you in your optimal state – energetic, productive, more resilient, and creative. When your battery is low, you may become more irritable, less patient with others and yourself, make more errors, and have difficulty connecting with others meaningfully.

ENERGY DRAINERS

- SOCIAL MEDIA
- COMPLAINING
- MULTITASKING

ENERGY FILLERS

- TAKING A WALK
- BEING ORGANISED
- SPORTS

- Reflect on at least **three activities that give you energy** throughout the day. It can be anything, such as taking a walk outside, engaging in sports, focusing on one task, celebrating small wins, meditating, or enjoying a hot drink in peace. Identify these activities and try to incorporate them into your daily or weekly routine to recharge your energy.
- Think of **three activities that drain your energy** and try to reduce them. For instance, you could spend less time on social media, try to complain less, or avoid multitasking and stressing about minor issues at work. Turning this into action will help you to manage your emotions, save your energy, and feel more positive throughout the day.

Scan the QR code to download the illustration and personalize it with your energy drainers and fillers.

Visualizing your energy drainers and energy fillers is a crucial step to taking action and being your own coach. It allows you to gain a better understanding and pro-actively redesign your approach (doing more, doing less, stopping, adapting, etc.).

Some of your energy fillers might even be a non-negotiable for your well-being.

IDEA 22

NON-NEGOTIABLE LIST FOR WELL-BEING

If you have daily or weekly habits that help you live your best life, then some of them might be non-negotiable for being the best version of yourself in general.

Here are some great examples of non-negotiables for your health, body and mind, applicable to having a great work week.

- Drinking a glass of water when you wake up
- Going for a short walk every day
- Stretching for five minutes at least once a day between meetings
- Meditating for X minutes early morning or during lunchtime
- Taking short breaks throughout the day to pause

- Reflecting on the highlight of the day
- Listening to a podcast episode/TEDx Talk
- Engaging in a sports activity at least X times a week

It is important to understand that non-negotiables vary from person to person. The key is to identify your own and prioritize them daily or weekly to experience their benefits.

Now, how to stick to it? That's a tricky question.

Sometimes, sticking to a new habit can be tough. But don't worry, it's not impossible.

The key is to make it a part of your daily routine, so it becomes effortless.

Let me share a personal example: I used to struggle to start my day with a glass of water. It might sound like an easy task, but I always seemed to forget amidst the morning chaos of getting my kids ready for school, preparing for early meetings, and thinking about the emails I needed to answer. Almost an hour and a half after I woke up, and I didn't have my glass of water. I decided to make it a "non-negotiable" for me and for my children. I kept reminding the whole family that drinking water first thing in the morning is so beneficial for our health and brain. I even explained the science behind it and had a sticky note on the fridge! After a few weeks of consistent effort (and by involving the whole family), it finally became a habit – not just for me, but for everyone at home.

Another strategy that has helped me maintain my non-negotiable list is adding reminders to my calendar. I usually schedule a short walk outside, especially on days filled with meetings or when I anticipate stressful days. Having a reminder ensures I follow through with it.

So, if you're looking to adopt a new habit, don't give up just yet. It's an ongoing practice. Keep reminding yourself about the benefits of your new habit, and try to make it a part of your daily routine. With time, you'll find that it becomes second nature and something that you won't even have to think about anymore.

If you're considering skipping a non-negotiable, ask yourself – *"How will I feel if I do?"*

In the end, no one should judge you; you are the one to decide!

While nurturing our own self-care helps create consistency in personal well-being, fostering a positive environment for self-care at work is equally powerful. Let's explore how companies can actively encourage employees to prioritize their well-being:

IDEA 23
ORGANIZE A SELF-CARE DAY FOR YOUR EMPLOYEES

The company Remote (Global HR Platform) is implementing a once-every-quarter self-care day for their employees. As they often communicated on LinkedIn:

> *Every quarter, we encourage everyone to take the day off and do something they love while we create awareness of the importance of self-care, mental health, and taking a break.*
>
> *– Remote*

Scan the QR code to see the post.

Get inspired by this initiative and customize it to fit your own culture. I've seen other companies implementing regular self-care breaks to boost morale and productivity. For instance, some offer a full or half-day break every month, while others provide extra time off to recharge after intense work periods, like meeting a deadline or completing a project. It's important that these breaks are offered regularly, not just once a year, to maintain effectiveness.

The objective of this initiative is not to provide more time for household chores but mostly to encourage people to engage in activities that they enjoy and have a positive impact on their well-being (reading a book, taking the time to listen to a podcast, just chilling in the garden, going for a long walk, etc.).

Some companies encourage employees to share pictures on their internal communication platform, creating a positive example and reducing guilt around taking self-care days.

The idea of organizing self-care days can be a wonderful way to incorporate self-care into your company's values. Make sure to adapt the format to your company's needs. Keep in mind that depending on your industry or company culture, the examples above might not make sense or be possible to apply. The key is to find a format that works for you; you might even include your employees in the process to find the right approach for everyone.

IDEA 24
CREATE A NETWORK OF WELL-BEING CHAMPIONS WITHIN YOUR COMPANY

Company Spotlight – Sonova – by Nadine Pietzonka

To exemplify this initiative, I have chosen to showcase Sonova, a company specializing in hearing care solutions, along with the efforts of their Senior Manager Corporate Health, Nadine Pietzonka.

Nadine explains how the company integrated well-being initiatives into its corporate culture and business strategies and how she engaged the well-being champions on a global level.

> When I began my new role as the Senior Manager Corporate Health at Sonova in 2022, my key goal was to lead global corporate well-being initiatives and begin creating a well-being strategy roadmap for the Sonova Group. I started by developing a model with four pillars: Creating Awareness, Enabling our People, Building Well-Being Communities, and Governance to bring the recently created holistic well-being framework with its five dimensions of well-being – Physical, Social, Mental, Financial, and Purpose – to life at Sonova. Utilizing our four strategic pillars and the five dimensions of well-being, we initiated the development of our roadmap and the implementation of well-being initiatives.

We have chosen to focus our local initiatives on physical, social, and financial well-being, as we can adapt and personalize the content to fit every country and culture. Our global initiatives mainly focus on the other two dimensions: purpose and employee mental health.

To lead and promote our local initiatives, we have created a global HR network of well-being enthusiasts, whom we call our Sonova well-being champions. They received assets from the headquarters to support the execution of global initiatives and have the flexibility to adapt those to the local environment while also leading local initiatives. For example, in one country, they decided to focus more on physical well-being and organized local awareness sessions on nutrition and sports. In another country, their main focus was on social well-being as they needed to boost group cohesion.

Our employees have extremely diverse roles, including operational, retail, sales, production, and office-based positions, and our initiatives need to be adjusted to suit their needs.

To ensure that we stay connected with our well-being champions and keep them informed and trained, we utilize various communication channels and platforms and hold bi-monthly 50-minute calls. These calls are recorded and focus on the following:

- Providing updates and information from headquarters regarding our well-being strategy.
- Facilitating best practices sharing among the champions, we like to call these moments "Steal with Pride." This is an opportunity to be inspired by others and celebrate successes.
- Discussing obstacles and challenges faced during the implementation of initiatives in order to gain support and learn from each other.

In addition to being active with our 70 well-being champions, we have also been working on improving the company's culture with various measures to enhance employee well-being. This includes setting shorter meeting durations automatically (25/50/80 minutes), training leaders in mental health first aid, offering our resilience programs such as 'Your Inner Strength' and 'Setting Boundaries,' and providing leadership development training on topics like meaningful conversations.

Tracking our impact is an important part of our strategy to achieve lasting results. It helps us to take action and react accordingly. For example, we have the following measurements:

- *Global annual employee engagement survey, including a separate well-being score, which will help local champions identify specific actions*
- *Monthly Pulse Check: We send a few short questions to a sample population to answer*
- *Number of participants in our well-being initiatives*
- *NPS (Net Promoter Score) for all programs*
- *Impact of our training through surveys after each session in which we also ask questions to assess impact and transfer to real life, for example: "How confident do you feel to apply what you have learned?" or "How confident are you now to start a conversation with another team member about mental health?"*
- *RVTO (Regrettable Voluntary TurnOver): We track the number of voluntary departures and try to understand the reasons behind them.*

We are working on a strong well-being culture within the company, but we still face some challenges. We need to find ways to engage our champions more regularly and ensure they receive the recognition they deserve.

Getting everyone on board can also be a challenge, but it's crucial. We encourage our executives to lead by example and actively support our initiatives, making sure that employee well-being stays a top priority in the company strategy. It's an ongoing process, and the key is to consistently work on it.

– Nadine Pietzonka, Senior Manager Corporate Health Sonova

There are many ways to structure and engage well-being champions within a company. What stands out about Sonova's approach is that it goes beyond simply coordinating well-being initiatives. The company has integrated well-being into the core of its strategy, implementing measures on a global scale. This approach highlights the importance of addressing well-being at the cultural level, ensuring that it becomes an integral part of the organization's identity and long-term success.

The crucial part of such an extensive and globally integrated strategy is the commitment and engagement of the top leadership. Without strong support and role-model behavior from leaders, employees might attach less value to such programs as it does not align with their business objectives.

IDEA 25

START A
WELL-BEING CAMPAIGN

Organizing a communication campaign focused on well-being is essential for companies aiming to foster a supportive and healthy work culture. When companies actively communicate their commitment to well-being, it not only increases awareness but also demonstrates that employees' health and happiness are prioritized. Such campaigns can bridge the gap between intention and action by promoting resources, sharing success stories, and normalizing conversations around mental health, resilience, and self-care. By making well-being a visible and ongoing topic, companies encourage employees to take advantage of available initiatives and feel more empowered to prioritize their own well-being, ultimately contributing to a more engaged and productive workforce.

I will first showcase two examples of companies and then summarize how to start a well-being campaign. You can adapt the steps and content to your needs.

For our first example, let's consider a multinational insurance company that formed a task force consisting of members from various departments (learning and development, change management, communication, marketing, compensation) to develop the company's strategy on mental health, well-being, and resilience.

As they started interviewing employees to assess their mental health, the task force discovered unexpected fears and challenges. For instance, many employees found it difficult to take a proper break during weekends or holidays because they received work emails and felt obligated to respond. Others mentioned that it was challenging to speak up or say no. Many employees also expressed discomfort in sharing their mental health status and seeking support.

The task force realized the importance of addressing these issues and decided to launch the campaign "It's okay to …"

They launched different messages monthly and began communicating their campaign through town hall meetings and various communication channels.

Their first messages focused on the following statements and intentions:

- ○ *"It's okay not to be okay"* – to bring importance to all their emotions and reduce stigma
- ○ *"It's okay to set boundaries"* – to bring more awareness on burnout and stress
- ○ *"It's okay to say no"* – to manage workload
- ○ *"It's okay to be who you really are"* – to celebrate Pride month and promote Diversity, Equality and Inclusion
- ○ *"It's okay to take a break"* – to encourage taking short breaks during workdays and reduce the pressure of checking emails during holidays

The messages used in this campaign helped employees become more aware of their mental health, receive more support, and feel less pressured, and sparked conversations within teams. It's a positive way to incorporate mental health, well-being, and resilience into the company's culture.

For example, closer to the summer holidays, the company launched the campaign "It's okay to take a break." The purpose of this campaign was to raise awareness about mental health and encourage employees to take a genuine break during their holidays. Leaders used this campaign to lead by example and create a positive influence. Employees felt much better during their holidays because they didn't have the pressure of checking their emails, answering business phone calls, or working on a project.

Other companies have different mental health or well-being campaigns that aim to promote a "speak up" culture. For instance, a global bank launched the "Dare to Decline" campaign to overcome the workload and fear of saying no.

Another insurance company launched the "This Is Me" campaign inspired by the UK mental health initiative, which allows employees to share their own stories about anxiety, burnout, and challenges. This campaign promoted a culture where people were not afraid to share their own stories and show vulnerability.

Steps to start your mental health/well-being campaign:

➡ Have a dedicated team to work on the campaign: e.g., a communication team, task force, ambassadors, and champions.

- Define the objectives of the campaign: e.g., increasing awareness, providing support, promoting resources, reducing stigma.

- Analyze the main challenges, fears, and stressors employees are facing in terms of their mental health through interviews, surveys, or workshops. It will help to develop and adapt your key messages.

- Craft impactful messages depending on your objectives and current situation: It can be a mix of inspirational, hands-on, clear, fun, visual, and action-oriented messages.

- Have the executive team on board to act as role models to support the campaign. Underline why the campaign is important, and showcase your strategy based on facts and numbers about the impact of mental health.

- Use regular and different communication channels such as monthly meetings, town halls, leadership meetings, leader talks, digital signage, internal communication platforms, newsletters, 1:1, team meetings, workshops, and trainings.

- Follow up on the campaign and adapt: Engage the task force, measure success against the initial objectives, and analyze feedback to adjust if needed.

Such campaigns, when done well, can significantly improve the company's culture on many levels, including transparency, authenticity, reduced fear of speaking up, decreased guilt, and improved open communication and work relationships. Of course, it won't have the same effect if employees don't feel they are in a safe and positive enough work environment to be able to share. You need to have a good foundation in your company's culture if you want the message to be well received.

I've observed that many companies often begin implementing diverse initiatives to promote mental health and well-being, but then they seem to stop after a while. It can be challenging to maintain consistency, provide valuable content, and keep employees engaged. That's why it's crucial to have ambassadors, a task force, or a dedicated team to continue raising awareness, developing engagement, and focusing on these important topics – it will make a real difference. Additionally, as previously mentioned, having the management on board and leading by example will make a real difference. These kinds of initiatives should be part of the company's culture and not just a temporary, nice-to-have feature.

The next initiative is a great example of how bringing consistent awareness about these crucial topics supports inclusion, engagement, and sustainable impact.

IDEA 26

INTERNAL MENTAL HEALTH PODCAST

Company Spotlight – Sanofi – by Nick Bellinger

I had the opportunity to work for different divisions within Sanofi, a top ten global pharmaceutical company, and support them in many ways to foster a positive work culture. I learned about Nick Bellinger's podcast through one of my clients at Sanofi and thought it was a fantastic idea. I could not resist including him in this book to explain the story behind the internal Sanofi Podcast and the impact it has had.

Here is how Nick Bellinger, Learning Business Partner for the European Region of Sanofi, transformed a regular catch-up between three British employees into a global internal Mental Health Podcast.

I believe Nick's story showcases the power of starting small to achieve big!

> *For many years, I struggled with anxiety, self-confidence, and feeling like I did not fit in. I also felt nervous around my colleagues. Last year, I was diagnosed with ADHD. One day, our Health and Safety specialist, Lisa, asked if I was interested in becoming a Mental Health First Aider (MHFA). At first, I did not feel comfortable with the idea, but she believed in me. I started to see that it was exactly what I needed. Being an MHFA taught me a lot and allowed me to use my experiences to help others, as well as gain new knowledge about how well-being struggles showed up in a commercial setting. That remains to be a wonderful opportunity to give back to my colleagues to this day.*

When doing the MHFA training, I found myself surrounded by wonderful people at Sanofi who wanted to support people with their mental health. I was sitting with a couple of friends in the session, and we noticed that out of the 40 people attending this training, only three were men. This made us wonder why. Are men not courageous enough to talk about mental health and understand that our mental well-being does not need to be perfect? One of the male participants suggested starting a podcast to address men's mental health at Sanofi. We thought this would be a wonderful opportunity to raise more awareness on this topic and involve more men in the conversation.

To be honest, I was quite nervous about the idea because I did not feel comfortable sharing my mental health struggles with everyone at the company. But, despite feeling a bit shy at first, I decided to get on board.

In 2020, we started by having a Zoom call with just the three of us. We shared our stories, discussed our coping strategies, and talked about our challenges. We then posted the conversation on our internal social network at Sanofi in the UK.

The early shows were remarkably simple – just a basic conversation between three British guys with no production involved. That did not last long, though.

After a short period of time, word about the podcast spread, and my colleague Lisa, who had previously inspired me to become an MHFA, reached out to us again. She suggested that we should make the podcast available to our global colleagues outside of the UK. Lisa arranged an international guest for us, which gave us exposure and got us thinking about mental health outside of the UK. This transformed the podcast, shifting the focus from just us to engaging in meaningful conversations about mental health at Sanofi Global.

Eventually, my two original colleagues who co-hosted the podcast with me left the company, and I continued hosting it by myself. I began inviting top leaders, including the Global HR Director, Natalie Bickford, and even the CEO of Sanofi, Paul Hudson, to share their experiences, challenges, and significant decisions related to mental health.

I started to realize that we had a much larger audience, with colleagues from all over the world tuning in to our podcast. I made an effort to feature guests with diverse backgrounds, including both well-known leaders in the company and colleagues with compelling stories to share, even if they were not globally recognized. My guests came from different corners of the globe, highlighting the diversity within Sanofi. People did not feel alone anymore. They now had stories from other people to which they could relate.

As the podcast grew, I knew I could not manage everything on my own. I made an agreement with my team to dedicate only one hour of my working time per week to the podcast. I started recruiting other volunteers, including colleagues who helped with editing, graphics, and production.

Some of my colleagues in other countries started the same podcast in their local languages (we now have episodes in French, Portuguese, Spanish, and German). They created small podcast franchises, and we started to organize live versions of the show once a year, inviting external speakers, including subtitles and sign language interpreters, and even organizing a bigger event for World Mental Health Day.

From a small Zoom call among three British colleagues to a global podcast for the entire company, the impact of this podcast has surpassed my expectations. The podcast has enabled me to spotlight the different forms of mental health, highlight the importance of prevention, and give visibility to neurodiversity. Many employees have shared that the podcast has been incredibly helpful as it has increased awareness about mental health topics by sharing stories, recognizing burnout signs, and sharing best practices.

Our next goal is to make the podcast available to the public, not just to Sanofi employees. We are currently exploring ways to create a safe space for sharing Sanofi stories outside the company. But for now, it is a work in progress, as we all are!

*– Nick Bellinger, Learning Business Partner
for the European Region, Sanofi*

The key is to address well-being at all levels – individual, team, and organizational. Taking an approach that is both top-down and bottom-up will ensure that every layer of the organization contributes to and benefits from the well-being initiatives. By involving everyone from executives to frontline employees in the conversation and execution, the strategy becomes more inclusive and effective.

The topic of well-being is a vast topic, and this book is too short to highlight all initiatives and ideas based on all well-being dimensions, but, if needed, you will find more information and resources on my website (such as the well-being playbook from the World Well-Being Movement, examples of other initiatives, and different apps, articles, and podcasts) through scanning the QR code.

CHAPTER HIGHLIGHTS

✔

Mental health and well-being are fundamental for employee satisfaction, productivity, and retention. Companies that prioritize these areas build healthier, more engaged, and successful teams.

✔

Leaders who cultivate a vision, consider people's needs, and invest in positive relationships report better mental health outcomes in their teams.

✔

There is no one-size-fits-all approach – well-being strategies must be tailored to the unique needs of both the organization and its employees.

✔

It's important to remember that in order to measure your team's well-being, happiness, or engagement, you should not only focus on quantitative facts but also qualitative ones.

✔

Individual approaches are important, but their impact is maximized when supported by organizational-level initiatives that create a strong foundation for holistic well-being.

LET'S TAKE ACTION

➡ Write down one thing you can start doing to support your overall well-being and specify how you can make it a part of your daily work routine:

➡ What well-being initiatives, small or large, could you implement within your team or company starting today?

➡ What are the biggest obstacles to improving your well-being at work, and how can you address them?

Access additional resources by scanning the QR code.

YOUR THOUGHTS
YOUR JOURNEY

Capture your insights, ideas, and action steps as you make this journey your own.

4

CRAFTING A POSITIVE EMPLOYEE EXPERIENCE FROM THE BEGINNING

Your Employees Are Your Greatest Asset

Your culture is your brand – it is the most effective way to attract and retain top talent, which, in turn, shapes your customers' experiences. There is a deep connection between an organization's internal culture and its external reputation.

The internal culture of a company reflects its core values, principles, and behaviors. These internal aspects are reflected in how the company presents itself to the outside world – through its products, services, customer interactions, and overall brand image.

Want to retain top talent?
Make them feel wanted.

Creating a strong and attractive company brand and implementing effective onboarding practices are critical steps in enhancing the overall employee experience.

- ○ *Does your company have a good reputation?*
- ○ *How's the hiring process?*
- ○ *Are you involving the new hire in preboarding?*
- ○ *How do you manage their onboarding?*

Cultivating a positive work culture not only fosters a productive and engaging workplace but also plays a crucial role in attracting top talents.

The journey of an employee with your company begins long before their first day on the job. It starts the moment they first interact with your company – be it through your website or social media, exploring your values and sustainable engagement, seeking out referrals, or examining your products and services. At this stage, your employer branding faces its first test.

In the Gallup report *Gallup's Perspective on Creating an Exceptional On-boarding Journey for New Employees*[1], the following numbers give a clear message:

➡️ **Only 12% of employees** strongly agree their organization does a great job of onboarding new employees.

➡️ Employees with an exceptional onboarding experience are **2.6 times** as likely to be extremely satisfied with their place of work.

➡️ New employees typically take around **12 months** to reach their full performance potential within a role.

According to another survey from BambooHR in 2023 of 2,300 U.S. Workers[2]:

➡️ Employees who had effective onboarding feel up to **18 times** more commitment to their workplace.

➡️ **89% of employees** who underwent strong onboarding reported feeling highly engaged at work, leading to better overall job satisfaction and retention.

➡️ **91% of new hires** who received an effective introduction to company culture training feel connected to their workplace – compared to just **29%** who say their onboarding experience was lacking.

By focusing on brand attraction and refining your hiring and pre/onboarding processes, you can significantly improve the employee experience right from the start.

Let's first visualize the employee life cycle to help you identify key moments when you can effectively promote a positive image of your company. As you strategically implement the best practices for brand attraction, hiring, and pre/onboarding, you lay the groundwork for a rewarding employee experience that starts even before their official first day.

The Employee Life Cycle

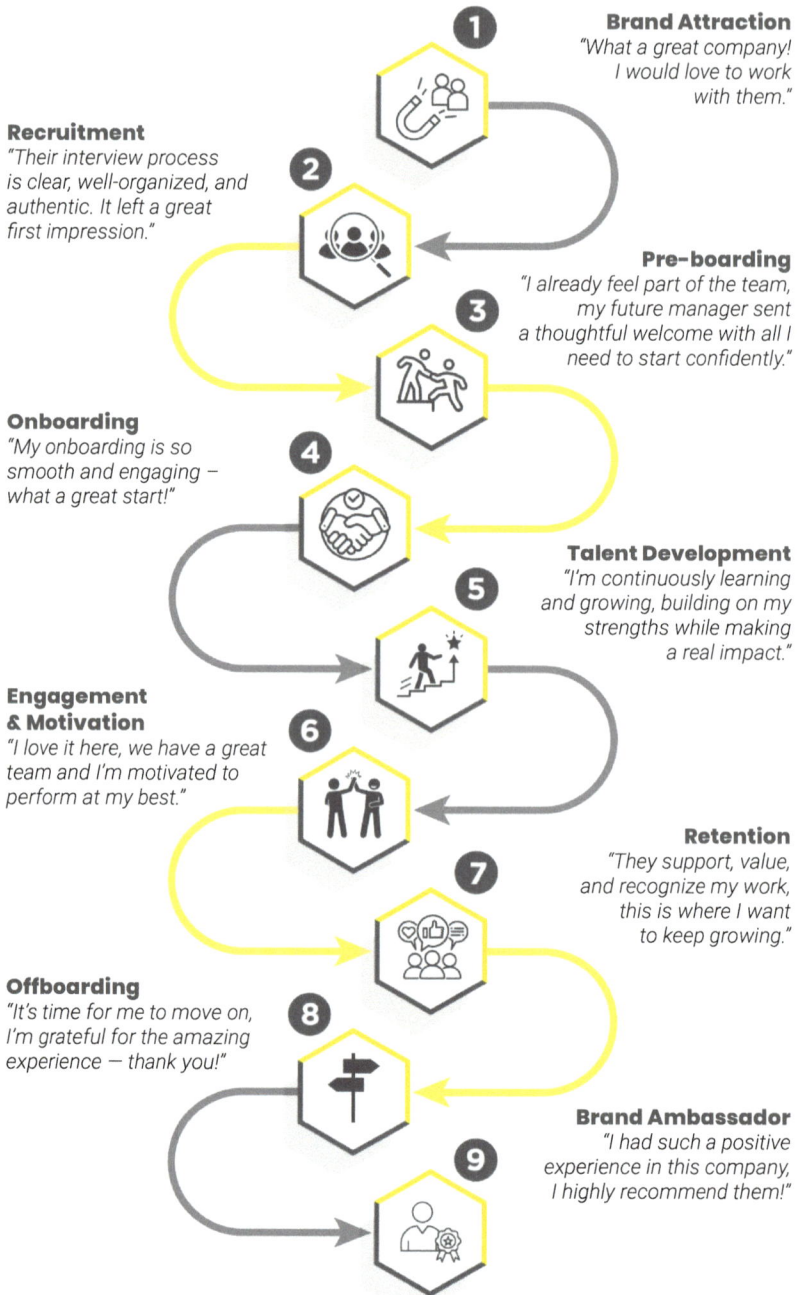

1 Brand Attraction
"What a great company!
I would love to work
with them."

2 Recruitment
"Their interview process
is clear, well-organized, and
authentic. It left a great
first impression."

3 Pre-boarding
"I already feel part of the team,
my future manager sent
a thoughtful welcome with all I
need to start confidently."

4 Onboarding
"My onboarding is so
smooth and engaging –
what a great start!"

5 Talent Development
"I'm continuously learning
and growing, building on my
strengths while making
a real impact."

**6 Engagement
& Motivation**
"I love it here, we have a great
team and I'm motivated to
perform at my best."

7 Retention
"They support, value,
and recognize my work,
this is where I want
to keep growing."

8 Offboarding
"It's time for me to move on,
I'm grateful for the amazing
experience — thank you!"

9 Brand Ambassador
"I had such a positive
experience in this company,
I highly recommend them!"

This chapter provides tools for employees and leaders in culture and human resources departments to create a positive impact at the beginning of the employee life cycle.

Creating a positive experience right from the start will make new employees great ambassadors. I've selected ideas you can implement and adapt to make sure you attract and include your talents from the beginning. I will be highlighting different initiatives from companies, such as Zühlke and L'Oréal, and I have also interviewed Ramona Sturzenegger, Chief People and Culture Officer at JobCloud, to share her expertise and strategy regarding employer branding and their employee life cycle.

Everything Starts Way Before Day 1

Even before hiring a new employee, a lot happens in terms of your employer brand and culture. Crafting the best experience can make a difference in your efforts to attract top talent and make them want to join your team not just for the salary but for the overall environment.

IDEA 27

STANDING OUT TO ATTRACT TALENT

Many companies highlight their culture through a brief brand introduction video or by being active on social media, offering viewers a snapshot of their business and company's culture. Make your brand introduction video or campaign authentic and memorable, ensuring it attracts top talent and conveys a positive company image. Let's move away from long, boring videos with monotonous voice-overs or cheesy videos where everyone looks overly enthusiastic and fake happy.

A company can truly differentiate itself by investing effort and involving employees to showcase its culture. Having employees share what they truly enjoy about their jobs and what they do in a modern way makes a significant impact.

Scan the QR code at the end of the chapter to explore selected examples of introduction videos and social media campaigns.

IDEA 28

SPICE UP THE WORDING IN YOUR JOB AD

Using the appropriate language style in your job ads is crucial. It should align with your company's culture and the position's profile. If you aim to stand out, project a modern image, and if you're looking to particularly attract younger generations, consider adapting your language style.

In addition, opting for inclusive language and gender-neutral terms will help attract talent and build a more diverse and inclusive workplace.

When you can, step away from the conventional format:
- *Key Responsibilities*
- *Key Requirements*
- *He or She*
- *Your Profile*
- *Skills Required*
- *What We Offer*

Explore and be inspired by these alternative phrases I sourced from different job ads – some of them even added some emojis in their posts to make the sentences stand out:
- *Your mission, should you choose to accept it*
- *This is what you bring to the table*
- *You'll be a great fit if you bring a few of the following with you:*
- *More than just a job*
- *What's in it for you?*
- *Your "super-power" tasks*

Here are three additional examples that are recommended by the Swiss recruitment platform JobCloud:

➡ **Employ purpose-driven language:** Connect the role to the company's broader mission and societal impact. Instead of simply describing tasks, use language such as: *"Your work will play a pivotal role in revolutionizing how we [insert company mission], helping us to make a real difference in [industry/society]."*

➡ **Use active and inviting language:** Replace passive phrases with active language that energizes the reader. Instead of *"Candidates must have experience in,"* try *"You'll bring your expertise in …"* This makes the ad feel more personal and appealing.

➡ **Engage with questions:** Pose questions to engage the reader. For example, *"Are you passionate about [industry/field]? Do you thrive in a dynamic environment where innovation meets execution?"* This invites the candidate to imagine themselves in the role.

IDEA 29
ENHANCING INTERVIEWS WITH EMOTIONAL INTELLIGENCE & CULTURAL FIT

In today's rapidly evolving workplace, the traditional interview process is undergoing a significant transformation. The importance of not only assessing a candidate's technical skills but also understanding their emotional intelligence (EI) and ensuring a mutual fit with the company's culture cannot be overstated.

By integrating EI considerations and open discussions about the company's culture into the interview process, organizations are able to identify not only candidates who are technically competent but also those who are likely to thrive and contribute positively to the workplace community. Consider personality, values, and communication style to determine their fit with the company or team's culture.

Ideas to apply during interviews to enhance the candidate experience

➡ Speak about the company's culture and explain proactively the company's initiatives related to mental health, employees' well-being, and continuous learning. It will give the candidate a better overview of the supportive environment they will be joining, highlighting the company's commitment to employee growth and well-being.

➡ Evaluate their emotional intelligence and human skills, not only their technical ones. Here are five EI questions you could ask the candidates:

- ○ *Tell me about a time when your mood had an impact on your work. (This could be positively or negatively.)*
- ○ *How do you celebrate your small wins at work?*
- ○ *How do you respond when a coworker challenges you?*
- ○ *What kind of behavior makes you angry/annoyed in the workplace?*
- ○ *How do you de-stress after a challenging day at work?*

These questions will help assess their self-awareness, self-regulation, social awareness, and ability to manage social interactions. You can refer to Chapter 6 on Emotional Intelligence to learn more about the topic.

➡ Evaluate what will boost the candidate's happiness level at work by asking questions such as:

- ○ *What makes you happy at work?*
- ○ *What's important for you in the workplace?*
- ○ *What would your ideal team look like?*

Discuss what creates positive emotions at work and their definition of happiness at work (refer to Chapter 1 for more info).

➡ Be transparent about the hiring process: What are the steps? How long would it take? Many companies express this up front (already in the job ad or the first interview), which is always a great way to manage the candidate's expectations.

➡ Make sure the candidate fits with your company's values and culture. The hiring manager can ask questions about how the candidate interprets and sees the company's values and how they would incorporate them into everyday situations. e.g.:

- *What does [company value, e.g., customer focus] mean to you, and how have you demonstrated commitment to this value in your previous work environment?*
- *Our company emphasizes [company value, e.g., diversity and inclusion or passion]. How have you incorporated such a value into your previous job roles?*
- *Tell us about a time when you took initiative in a project or task. What motivated you, and what was the impact of your actions on your team or the company?*

These questions are crafted to uncover responses that provide deeper insights into how well the candidate's personal values and behaviors align with those of your company, ensuring a cultural fit that facilitates both individual and organizational success.

Next, let's look at some best practices once you've made a new hire.

Elevate the Preboarding Experience

It's a common concern among new hires that they often experience a communication gap from the point of being hired to their first day. Can you imagine the uncertainty they might encounter during the intermediate weeks? The absence of interaction can make the new recruit feel isolated or even question their decision.

On the other hand, an effective preboarding process ensures new employees are kept in the loop from the time they accept the offer until their commencement. This proactive approach fosters enthusiasm and a sense of community, greatly enhancing new hire retention and minimizing the chance of any last-minute change of heart.

In addition to providing a nice welcome package and efficiently managing administrative tasks before their first day, try these engaging and fun ideas during your preboarding process:

IDEA 30

SPARK CURIOSITY WITH A CULTURE BOOKLET

Captivate your new hires by sending them your company's culture booklet or onboarding booklet in advance. Craft fun culture manuals or even a comic book to express the company's culture, main values, working style, and overview of products/services. It can be a fun and creative way to inform the new candidate about the company.

This type of booklet is not only for newcomers but can also be valuable for employees who relocate to a new city or country. Sharing tips and recommendations and introducing the new office in a fun and informative way can make a real difference in helping them feel included from the beginning while adding a personal touch. This kind of booklet should regularly be updated to reflect any changes in the company's culture or values.

Scan the QR code for some examples of cool culture booklets.

IDEA 31

INVOLVE NEW HIRES EARLY

Onboarding doesn't have to begin on day one. By involving new hires early, you can help them feel welcomed, valued, and connected even before they officially join the team. Here are some simple ways to create a smooth and engaging preboarding experience that fosters a sense of belonging from the start.

➡ Arrange a virtual or in-person meet and greet with their future colleagues once they've been hired. The discussion will be different and more authentic than during the interview process.

➡ Ask three (more personal) questions about the new employees to be able to inform the team about the new hire. Sharing details such as who they are, future roles, and the projects they will be involved in. I especially like the idea of sending a brief video (check the QR code) or a short portrait of the new hire, where they introduce themselves in just a few minutes. It's a great way to shape their first impression!

For some people, or depending on the company's industry, sending a video of themselves without even first meeting the team or during their first weeks at work might be uncomfortable. At the company Zühlke, they had this exact situation, as Lena Bass, Regional Lead Employer Branding DACH, explains:

> At Zühlke, we used to do videos with new joiners. The existing staff liked them very much; however, for the joiners, it was a lot of stress, and they did not appreciate having to record a video during their very first couple of days with the company. We had to change our strategy. What we do now is publish a little joiner's portrait, where we ask a couple of questions about who they are, what's their future role with us, and one random question to get to know them better, and this works really well. We ask them to fill this out before they join so we can introduce them while they're going through our onboarding program.
>
> – Lena Bass, Regional Lead Employer Branding DACH at Zühlke

➡ Include the new hire in possible social events during the preboarding process. This will strengthen connections within the team even before they officially start and enhance their integration.

IDEA 32

SEND A CANDIDATE EXPERIENCE SURVEY

Asking for feedback on their recruitment signals the shift from potential employee to team member. It gives the chance to collect immediate thoughts that could improve the hiring process, and on top of that, it might include the new hire from the start.

Examples of information you could source from the candidate to find out how their job interview went:

- ○ *The application form was simple to fill out*

  ☆ ☆ ☆ ☆ ☆

- ○ *I was provided with accurate information about the company and the recruitment process*

  👍 👍 👍 👍 👍

- ○ *The recruiter made me feel comfortable*

  🤟 🤟 🤟 🤟 🤟

- ○ *The recruiter had a good understanding of the job role and the company*

  💪 💪 💪 💪 💪

- ○ *I feel satisfied with the overall recruitment process*

  😠 🙁 😐 🙂 😄

- ○ *I would suggest for next time to...*

Obtain a complete Candidate Experience Survey Template by scanning the QR Code.

IDEA 33

INSPIRE EMPLOYEES TO LEARN BEFORE DAY 1

Give them access to your learning platform, personality test, or strength analyses, ensuring participation is entirely voluntary. Providing early access to your learning platform allows the employees to familiarize themselves with the tool and develop their technical and human skills before Day 1 if needed or desired. It's a great way to elevate the new hire's strengths and avoid a skill gap. If sharing your learning platform before their first day is impossible, companies can be creative by sharing public online courses, business book recommendations, or free webinars.

An Efficient Onboarding Is Structured and Fun!

An effective onboarding shouldn't be for just one day or even a few days if you are lucky! The first year of the employee is crucial.

It's important to have a structured plan for new hires and check on them regularly in their first year. A successful onboarding strategy will reduce employee turnover and increase engagement. Adding some fun initiatives for them to connect easily with others will help their integration phase.

IDEA 34

CULTURE IMMERSION FROM THE BEGINNING

Company Spotlight – L'Oréal – by Justyna Pytel

In addition to sharing the culture book in advance (as previously explained), organizing onboarding events and trainings to explain and demonstrate the company's culture, vision, mission, and core values will make a huge difference. Some companies use interactive tools and gamification, such as quizzes, to make the onboarding and learning process fun and engaging. This helps new hires remember the information easily and enjoyably.

Joining a mentoring program from the start can help new employees better understand the company culture and feel supported, heard, and included. This fosters a sense of belonging and speeds up their integration and evolution into the company.

I am still amazed to hear how many new employees had lunch alone on their first day because their colleagues didn't even know they were starting or were busy with meetings and other plans. Planning a lunch well in advance with an assigned colleague will make the first-day experience much better!

L'Oréal, the world leader in beauty, has implemented the FIT Program to ensure that new employees meet different people and feel included during their first year of onboarding. I asked Justyna Pytel, Head of People Development and Learning at L'Oréal, to explain their FIT Program:

> *L'Oréal has created a special onboarding ritual called FIT. A FIT is basically an informal meeting or get-together between two employees who haven't met before – usually a new employee and another colleague:*
>
> → *The newcomer's manager is responsible for providing a FIT roadmap with an initial list of key people the newcomer should meet: peers, cross-functional stakeholders, global community, typically around 10– 15 individuals to meet during the first month or two in the company.*
>
> → *On the other hand, the newcomer is responsible for actively reaching out to these individuals in the first few months and asking for a FIT (lasting between 30 and 45 minutes).*
>
> *It promotes empowerment, growth mindset, and "L'Oréalization" from the start. Proactively scheduling FITs with total strangers, regardless of hierarchy, is a great way to dive into L'Oréal's informal, inspiring culture. FITs are a key part of our daily routine, and anyone invited will gladly make time for it – it's an essential and refreshing part of our calendars!*
>
> *During a FIT, people introduce themselves authentically – whether chatting about hobbies over coffee, sharing their L'Oréal journey on Teams, or present- ing a few slides about their work. Regardless of the format, it's a powerful way to spark curiosity, inclusivity, and growth.*
>
> *The benefits of FITs are numerous, and newcomers love them:*
>
> *They start building a meaningful internal network, crucial for a successful career at L'Oréal, fostering synergies, best practices, and innovation.*
>
> → *They get familiar with the company's interconnected and complex structure.*
>
> → *They make a strong first impression, gain visibility, and showcase their ambitions.*

➡️ *Managers gather valuable feedback from FIT participants, helping identify the potential of new joiners.*

The FIT roadmap never ends because onboarding at L'Oréal never really ends either. Once the mandatory FITs are done, the newcomer must expand their connections further and further, based on recommendations, scope of work, personal flair, etc. Networking is fully part of our employees' performance and development goals. It honors our founder Eugene Schueller's most famous quote: "A company is not about walls and machines but about people, people, people."

99
— Justyna Pytel, Head of People Development and Learning, L'Oréal

IDEA
35
ONBOARDING BINGO

Onboarding bingo is a top choice for welcoming new hires with interactive elements and humor. It includes fun tasks that new members must complete to learn about their new team in the coming weeks. Once the bingo is completed, they will feel satisfied that they have learned much more about the culture and people in the company, and maybe even receive a small reward from the HR department!

This game will strengthen relationships and allow new hires to discover and discuss more with their colleagues and the company. Scan the QR code at the end of this chapter to download the PDF format.

ONBOARDING BINGO

Took a 10 minute walk with a new colleague	Had lunch with my team	My adventure starts today!	All my devices are finally working	Shadow a teammate for 30 minutes
Heard "can everyone see my screen"	Posted my bingo progress in team chat	Expressed my opinion and expertise	Had lunch with a colleague from another department	Met a colleague outside of work
Completed a training on the learning platform	Participated in my first client meeting	**BINGO**	Learned about one company tradition	Attended my first social event
Set one goal for my first 30 days	Received feedback from the team	Did a random act of kindness	Called a colleague for advice	Learned about one company tradition
Had a 1:1 with my manager	Presented a project / an idea	Used my networking skills	Met an executive from another department	Sent a message in the team chat channel

IDEA 36

ALLOCATE A BUDDY FOR THE ONBOARDING

This one is quite self-explanatory. However, let's see what a buddy can do to make a real difference in the new hire onboarding experience. Many companies are still missing the opportunity to support their new talent with a buddy or accountability partner.

A buddy's main goals might include:

➡ Introducing new talent to the team.

➡ Guiding the newcomer through everyday tasks.

➡ Including them in social activities/networking events.

➡ Helping with any queries or challenges related to the job or company.

➡ Explaining or showing the behind-the-scenes from the company (I'm not necessarily talking about all the drama and gossip but more about the information that you do not include in the culture book).

➡ Organizing regular 1:1s to follow up on the onboarding process (minimum for the first three months, ideally for a year).

Offering such support significantly impacts the new hire by fostering confidence and relationships with others. An onboarding buddy is often someone from the same team, who can differ from a mentor or a coach.

IDEA 37

NOURISH YOUR RELATIONSHIPS LIKE YOUR PLANTS

Let me share an idea my husband had; he used to offer every new team member a small tree, such as a lemon or lime tree. His message was that a team should grow together, and we must nourish relationships between colleagues, just like watering our plants.

Plus, there's a fun twist: They can use the limes for drinks after work!

To foster trust, collaboration, and unity right from the start, it's important to establish a strong rapport with colleagues by demonstrating kindness, offering support, listening actively, giving recognition, and maintaining open communication.

Good relationships take effort to maintain, just like a plant needs consistent care to thrive. By investing time and energy into nurturing these connections, you're not just building a team – you're cultivating a community. As your relationships grow, so will the strength and success of your collective efforts. Remember: the roots you establish today will support your team for years to come.

NOURISH YOUR RELATIONSHIPS

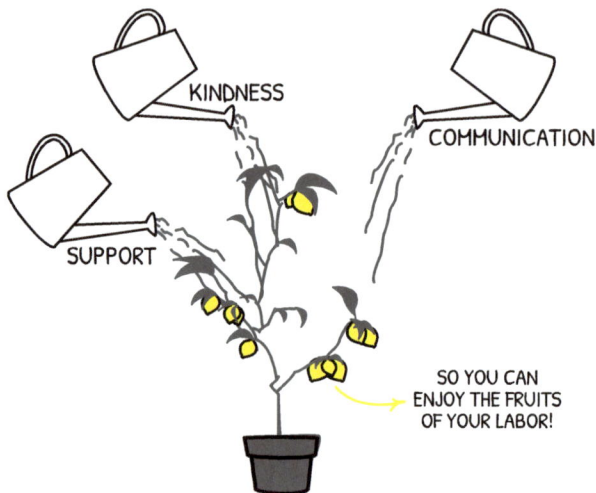

KINDNESS

COMMUNICATION

SUPPORT

SO YOU CAN ENJOY THE FRUITS OF YOUR LABOR!

Best Practices for Strong Employer Branding and Positive Employee Experience

Interview with Ramona Sturzenegger, Chief People & Culture Officer at JobCloud

I have been following the company JobCloud (a leading digital company in the Swiss job market) for a few years now and have had opportunities to support them for several initiatives. Their employer branding has developed a lot over the years, and I have used their examples many times to show a positive and strong employer branding.

I have interviewed Ramona Sturzenegger, Chief People & Culture Officer at JobCloud, to get insights on their employer branding strategy and how they ensure a smooth employee experience:

Aurelie Litynski: *JobCloud is very active in employer branding, particularly on social media, where many employees use their personal accounts to promote the company. What is your employer branding strategy, and what are your main challenges in maintaining a strong presence?*

Ramona Sturzenegger: *Our strategy for employer branding at JobCloud revolves around authenticity, transparency, and engagement. We strive to present a genuine picture of what it's like to work here, showcasing our values and culture through various communication channels. This includes a compelling company intro video, thematic social media campaigns like the one for Mother's Day (the thousand jobs of our mothers), and external webinars accessible to all (employees, clients, and external).*

We cultivate a work culture that encourages employees to promote JobCloud by fostering pride and a sense of belonging. We involve employees in our initiatives, celebrate their achievements publicly, and provide platforms for them to share their stories. Social media training and internal communication channels help employees feel confident and empowered to act as brand ambassadors. By maintaining a transparent and inclusive environment, we ensure that employees are genuinely enthusiastic about sharing their positive experiences with their networks.

Our primary challenge is maintaining consistency and relevance in our messaging, ensuring it resonates with both current and potential employees. Keeping up with the evolving expectations of the workforce and integrating their feedback into our branding efforts is also crucial.

Aurelie: *How do you ensure culture fit during the recruitment process?*

Ramona: *Our interview process is designed to assess both technical competencies and cultural fit. We employ behavioral and situational questions that help us understand how candidates align with our core values. Candidates have an opportunity to interact with potential future colleagues without the presence of a manager to get a sense of the day-to-day life at JobCloud. After this step, applicants typically complete a trial day or a business case, which they must solve and present. We intentionally involve different colleagues in this process to assess the applicant's professional and cultural fit from multiple perspectives, reflecting our company values.*

We also work with psychological online tests, which provide us with empirical results and generally confirm what we have already observed. Behavioral tendencies play a significant role in determining cultural fit. We are transparent about the test results and discuss any deviations with the candidate.

If we reject the candidate, we always do this personally and don't give "simple rejections" but rather transparent feedback on what didn't fit. We give tips on how the candidate can do better in the next interview. We greatly appreciate the candidates' performance and the time spent on the trial day or business case development. As a thank-you gift for their involvement and interest, we always plant a tree for them through our partner for global reforestation.

Aurelie: *What initiatives are you implementing to enhance an optimal employee experience at JobCloud?*

Ramona: *We have several initiatives to ensure a seamless transition for employees at every stage. The preboarding process includes virtual tours, introductory videos, a JobCloud welcome package, and at least 2–3 check-ins* *with the manager even before their first day. During onboarding, we provide remote onboarding sessions, comprehensive training sessions, cross-departmental meet-and-greets, and personalized trial period plans.*

Throughout their employment, we conduct regular training on psychological safety, provide resources for mental health support, and encourage open dialogue through initiatives like anonymous feedback channels and regular one-on-one check-ins with managers. Moreover, we offer a range of professional development opportunities, 360° feedback, and flexible working arrangements. Special initiatives throughout the year, such as the Week of Happiness at Work and mentorship programs, help our employees grow their skills and stay motivated and engaged.

We emphasize as well on salary transparency, providing clear career ladders for growth and development. Our open CEO talks, where employees can define the topics they want to discuss with the CEO once a month, further reinforce our commitment to open communication.

Such cultural touchpoints regularly occur throughout the entire life cycle of an employee, right up to offboarding with a farewell package.

For offboarding, we focus on exit interviews to gather feedback, send a JobCloud farewell package to close the circle, and maintain positive relationships, which often leads to boomerang employees (workers returning to a former employer) or strong ambassadors for JobCloud.

– Ramona Sturzenegger, Chief People & Culture Officer, JobCloud

This example of how JobCloud has implemented a full strategy on their company's brand and employee experience shows the great importance certain companies give to these topics. Employees are the most important resource and also a high investment for every company. Making sure that they have a positive experience within the company and that they convey their impressions to the outside world in an authentic and motivating way can leverage the large information spread such personal voices provide.

It is clear that such an elaborate strategy does not arise in the short term. Companies, rather, grow their approaches over time and complement them with new ideas that are being tested in real life.

CHAPTER HIGHLIGHTS

✔

Cultivating a positive work culture not only fosters a productive
and engaging workplace but also plays a crucial role
in attracting and retaining top talent.

✔

The journey of an employee with your company
begins long before their first day on the job.

✔

Including the new hire in your team even before their first day
can be done easily and has many advantages.

✔

Implementing a structured onboarding process is key.

✔

Create positive experiences all along the employee life cycle, from brand
attraction and recruitment to offboarding and brand ambassador.

✔

By investing time and energy into nurturing good relationships, you're not
just building a team, you're also cultivating a community.

LET'S TAKE ACTION

➡ Take a deep dive at your team's hiring process. Does it support hiring goals and the company's culture?

➡ Ask recent hires about their experience; what's their feedback?

➡ How can you contribute to creating a positive experience for newly hired colleagues in your current role?

Access additional resources by scanning the QR code.

YOUR THOUGHTS
YOUR JOURNEY

Capture your insights, ideas, and action steps as you make this journey your own.

chapter

5

NURTURING
MEANINGFUL
WORKPLACE
RELATIONSHIPS

Can Our Colleagues Be Like a Second Family?

If you want to foster a human-centric culture within your team or company, the pillar of relationships at work is important. After all, most of us spend more day time with our colleagues (even virtually) than our family when we work in an office.

Many experts have told us that having a sense of belonging, getting along with our colleagues and managers, and showing gratitude, kindness, and respect will enhance our work relationships and trust.

But what does it mean to have good relationships at work?

And do we need our team members to be our best friends or like a second family?

In my opinion, there is no right or wrong answer here. We all define "good relationships" differently, and we all have different needs depending on our extroverted or introverted personalities. Some employees just want to come to work, do their jobs, and interact the least with others. Some love to come to the office and spend lots of time chatting with others. Socializing can be draining or uplifting! We are all different. But even so, when relationships are overall positive, it makes the experience more enjoyable for everyone involved.

I have been on teams with toxic leaders where I just wanted to get through the day and go back home, and I have been on teams that felt like a second family to me. With my extroverted personality, it's important for me to feel close to my colleagues and managers, especially as I have been working abroad since the beginning of my career and have been far away from my family since I was a young adult. Some of my former colleagues are now my best friends, and some of the leaders I've worked with have become my role models.

Building genuine relationships at work can be incredibly powerful for team-work, trust, and our sense of belonging.

**Having good relationships at work
doesn't mean agreeing with others all the time.**

One important aspect, regardless of our personality styles, is to establish appropriate boundaries, just as we would in any other relationship outside of work.

The Harvard Study of Adult Development, directed by Robert Waldinger, is one of the longest-running studies on happiness, having tracked the lives of participants for over 80 years. One of the most significant findings from this study is that meaningful relationships are a crucial factor in long-term happiness and health[1]. You can watch his TED Talk by scanning the QR code.

> *The people who were the most satisfied in their relationships at age 50 were the healthiest at age 80. Loneliness kills. It's as powerful as smoking or alcoholism.*
>
> *– Robert Waldinger, psychiatrist, Massachusetts General Hospital*

In this chapter, I've selected initiatives that will help you cultivate human connections at work, enhance best-practice sharing, have more fun in teams, and inspire you with a DEI initiative. You will find case studies from Salesforce and PMI, and other companies' initiatives to uplift relationships in your own team.

As we delve deeper into the value of relationships, it's essential to recognize how these connections can be maintained and strengthened, especially in our increasingly digital work environments.

Human Connections
Are Hard to Replace

Due to technology, human connections are becoming less frequent and, therefore, even more important. With the rise of robotics, artificial intelligence, and remote work, our relationships at work can suffer. In the end, I am a true believer that nothing can replace human connections. Having regular touchpoints and ongoing conversations in different formats will help foster meaningful relationships at work.

We are constantly communicating on messaging apps with colleagues, but we don't connect in the same meaningful way as we would around a cup of coffee. Worse, working in the office or from home, we jump from one conference call to another, but although we have humans on our screens, we don't make time to check in with them on a personal level. This can leave us feeling more drained and isolated.

I've selected five easy ways to connect on a deeper level with your colleagues:

IDEA 38

HAPPINESS TALKS

Unlike the typical 1:1 session we might have with our team members or colleagues to discuss projects or work-related matters, Happiness Talks are 1:1 catch-ups that prioritize emotional well-being. These conversations revolve around topics other than work, focusing on the individual's overall well-being, energy levels, and personal life. I like to refer to them as "Happiness Talks" because the term serves as a reminder to connect on an emotional level first. You can also call them "Well-Being Chats" or whatever you prefer. The key is to prioritize emotional connection.

These talks help to build trust and show that you value your team members beyond their work contributions.

Here are examples of how to initiate Happiness Talks:

- *How do you feel lately?*
- *How's your energy level today?*
- *How's your family doing?*
- *Is your father recovering from [X]?*
- *Has anything been on your mind that you want to talk about?*

Showing genuine interest in how they feel and in their life outside of work will help to foster healthy and honest relationships at work. You might, of course, adapt the questions depending on the culture and personality of the person you are talking to. Some people prefer not to share anything related to their personal lives and this is something to be respected.

Think about your last meaningful conversation at work – what made it impactful?

IDEA 39

2-WORDS CHECK-IN

We often find ourselves jumping right into a meeting by talking about the project or the next task to accomplish without spending much time on proper greetings.

Taking a few minutes to ask your team members how they are feeling at the beginning of a meeting before diving into business topics can be very powerful. It also helps to take the mood temperature of the room.

My favorite questions for this kind of check-in are:

○ *Describe in two words how you are feeling right now, and feel free to explain why.*

Or, as an alternative:

○ *What kind of emotions do you have today and why?*

With these kinds of questions, you might hear answers like:

○ *Today, I'm feeling overwhelmed and anxious.*

○ *I'm feeling stressed and alone.*

○ *I'm proud and energized because we just launched our new campaign.*

○ *I honestly feel tired and angry because I didn't have a good night's sleep, and I received a negative answer from a client first thing this morning.*

○ *I feel a bit anxious and stressed about my presentation for this afternoon.*

Having honest answers requires a good level of psychological safety within the team. You can ask your team members if they want to elaborate further, allowing you to connect privately with your colleague if you feel the need to continue the conversation after the meeting.

Asking such questions at the beginning of a meeting or workshop is not a waste of time; in fact, it can make the meeting more productive. It helps employees feel safe and seen, enables colleagues to understand each other's state of mind better, and may lead to an adaptation of communication styles. It provides space for self-reflection and self-awareness, which can help individuals better own and regulate their emotions.

Keep in mind that it's not a one-size-fits-all, and it's not something you do every time you have a meeting; otherwise, some of us might answer this question every hour or two. You need to adapt the format, the question, and the frequency depending on the audience. It shouldn't take too long and can be done virtually using interactive tools or in-person meetings, paying attention to maintaining a good flow. Doing this kind of check-in with your team will foster better relationships and trust.

IDEA 40

QUICK CONNECT

"Quick Connects" are brief interactions that can be done in different ways: email, SMS, phone calls, or in person, such as at the coffee machine. Having quick connections with your team members or colleagues can help them stay on track, touch base, and provide support and encouragement.

A Quick Connect might involve passing a team member in the hallway and asking, *"By the way, what's the status of this project? Do you need my support on anything?"* Another example is sending an SMS to a team member who has an important review with the C-level, saying, *"Sending my good vibes for your meeting, you will rock it!"* Of course, the purpose of all these ongoing conversations should be genuine, adaptable and not feel forced.

IDEA 41

During one of my leadership programs, Leo, country leader in the health-care industry, shared with the group that he started to implement "Crucial Conversations" with his employees once or twice a year for high-potential individuals. This is neither a performance review nor a typical 1:1 catch-up. The goal of this Crucial Conversation is to take enough time to create a special moment for the employee, being fully present and creating a safe space for the person to share. It doesn't typically happen in the office; you can do it during a long walk around the office or at a special location for the occasion.

Here are important factors to pay attention to during this 1:1 Crucial Conversation:

→ Choose the right location and atmosphere.

→ Take enough time to be fully present for the employee.

→ No numbers or specific business cases.

→ Celebrate skills and competencies.

→ Highlight improvements, recognize their personal success, and make your people aware of their importance.

→ Ask for their long-term target and define the right pathway for the next 6–12 months.

→ Focus on emotions and reactions and create a fully trusted environment.

→ It's not about business but about them.

Taking the time to have deep conversations with your team members can make a real difference. This kind of conversation must be a special moment to remember for both parties.

IDEA
42

WALK & TALK

Not every meeting needs to take place in a meeting room or behind a screen. With our new way of working, we spend much more time sitting than we used to when we went to the office every day. I have noticed many people having online meetings, even when they are in the office and on the same floor. We are often missing out on opportunities to strengthen relationships, get moving, and get more creative. Especially for meetings that don't require showing a slide deck or sharing a screen, having a Walk-and-Talk meeting can be very effective. Being outside and active can make you more creative, making it the perfect format for brainstorming sessions.

It's also a great format if you need to have an important conversation with a team member. Walking and facing forward can make it easier for some people to have a deep conversation or share their feelings than sitting at a desk and looking into the person's eyes.

Creating connections is just the start; fostering a positive environment through small, meaningful interactions can further solidify these bonds.

Let's Break the Ice

How many times have you started a meeting feeling tension in the room or diving straight into the project? Breaking the ice before starting a meeting or a long session can reduce tension and social barriers among participants. It can help create a positive environment and encourage communication and collaboration.

So, do we need to break the ice every time we start a meeting? Maybe not, but from time to time, spending a few minutes to start on a positive note can make a real difference.

Research, including studies by Barbara Fredrickson, an American psychologist professor, and other experts, demonstrates that starting meetings with positivity can significantly enhance efficiency and creativity. Fredrickson's "broaden-and-build" theory[2] explains that positive emotions expand people's thinking and openness, fostering creativity and resilience.

In this section, I'll share different initiatives to help you break the ice in future meetings, conversations, or team dynamics:

IDEA 43

5 ICEBREAKERS TO START YOUR MEETING WITH POSITIVITY

Start your next meeting with a quick round where each person shares something positive. Depending on the group size, you can use interactive tools such as Mentimeter or Slido to collect answers and make groups of two or three. The goal is not to spend too much time on it.

You can pick one of these questions and let everyone share:

- *Name a person who has helped you since the last meeting and explain briefly why.*
- *Mention one thing you're looking forward to at work in the coming week.*
- *Share a compliment/give appreciation to a coworker.*
- *What's the funniest thing someone told you recently?*
- *Share your most recent accomplishment (big or small).*

Scan the QR code at the end of the chapter to be inspired by more icebreakers.

IDEA 44

5 DIFFERENT WAYS TO SPARK A CONVERSATION

We have become so used to the phrase *"Hi, how are you?"* that it has lost its meaning and become banal. Many times, we have been asked this question and felt like our responses were not truly listened to.

Here are five unique ways to enhance your next conversation:

- *What was your day like?*
- *What would make this a good conversation for you?*
- *What would you like to talk about and not talk about today?*
- *Did anything make you smile today?*
- *In one word, how would you describe your day?*

What I love about these is that they surprise people, and it makes them take a quick minute to think and reflect on their emotional state. It is a great way to help our colleagues connect with themselves and us.

IDEA 45

5 QUESTIONS TO SUPPORT YOUR TEAM'S GROWTH

Involving your teams in reflecting on what's working well, what could be improved, and what they learned can positively impact their performance.

Learning new things will not only make you smarter but also improve your engagement, performance, and adaptability. On top, it gives you a sense of progress, which can increase your happiness level.

The following questions are fantastic for team growth:

- *How do you think we are doing as a team?*

- *Is there anything we should adapt or change to thrive?*
- *What should we keep doing as a team?*
- *What have you/we learned recently?*
- *What sparked your curiosity lately?*

Be aware that this isn't just another story of the suggestion box that nobody reads. Your team will expect these discussions to be put to good use. If they bring issues that grab your attention, then you must do something about them. That's part of building trust and fostering a functioning team.

IDEA 46

LET'S SPIN THE WHEEL

As a child, I used to watch my grandmother's favorite TV game show with her, featuring a giant spinning wheel that won the contestants cash and prizes. It was, I believe, the French version of the famous American show *Wheel of Fortune*.

So, you can imagine how thrilled I was during the pandemic when I discovered that many online platforms had created spinning wheels to engage people in online meetings and make interactions more fun! It always brings me back to my childhood with a smile.

Using an online spinning wheel to engage people, answer questions, or choose an activity can be fun, efficient, and inclusive. You can create your own or use existing platforms to choose a question from. Scan the QR code for some examples.

Here are a few ideas on ways to utilize online roulette:

- To choose who is going to lead the discussion first
- To choose an icebreaker question
- To engage participants in sharing their points of view, feedback, or ideas
- To make a recognition round: when the name appears, this person will give appreciation, praise, or positive feedback to someone else

➡ To boost playfulness by getting to know each other better: e.g., when a name appears, the meeting leader will ask something about this person (it can be a personal question: *"What's her cat's name?"* or a professional question: *"Which client did this person gain recently?"*) and the others need to find the answer – this gives a fun twist as there is competition involved

➡ To choose topics for discussions

Beyond just connecting, there's immense value in learning from one another – leveraging each other's strengths to foster a culture of continuous growth.

Learn From Each Other – Explore Your Human Library

Sharing best practices has a positive impact on team performance, motivation, and efficiency. Learning from others can develop skills, enhance team cohesion, and build bonds. It creates an environment of transparency and collaboration, where employees are appreciated for their input and encouraged to gain knowledge from one another. This ultimately strengthens team unity and boosts morale. Think of all the potential we have in companies as a human library!

There are many ways to develop best-practice sharing in teams. I've selected three efficient initiatives that I find have a great impact.

IDEA 47 — LUNCH & LEARN SESSION

I have been invited to lead many lunch and learn sessions, and I love the informal concept and its impact. The idea behind a lunch and learn is to organize a short session (between 30 and 90 minutes) during or around lunchtime – a breakfast session could work as well. Participants get inspired and learn about a specific topic while networking and having lunch with their colleagues. The goal is to promote continuous learning and development in a relaxed, more casual setting that encourages engagement and discussion. These sessions are usually held by an external speaker, a company leader, or an employee who shares a special skill.

The topics vary from learning technical or human skills, sharing their best tips on a specific topic, or even sharing lessons learned after making a mistake.

IDEA 48

SKILL SWAP SESSION

Unlike the lunch-and-learn sessions, which might be organized by the team or the company itself, the skill swap sessions are usually organized by company volunteers. Sometimes, we don't even realize that one of our colleagues is an expert in a specific skill.

For example, imagine your colleague Thomas is good at public speaking because, during his free time, he is part of a local Toastmasters group (an international non-profit organization that teaches public speaking). Thomas could lead a skill swap session to share his best tips on public speaking, which could benefit the participants for their next presentation.

In return, someone else might share their expertise in Excel, PowerPoint, coding, or teaching others an instrument or breathing techniques. We all have qualities and strengths that people don't always know about. It's a fantastic way to give and learn from each other. This can be done face-to-face or virtually.

IDEA 49

TEAM ERASMUS PROGRAM

You might have heard about the well-known European Erasmus program, which allows students to study in another country for a few months during their education.

A leader I have been working with had the idea to organize a Team Erasmus program for his international sales team. They needed to get to know each other better, learn from each other, and develop team cohesion. The idea was to send an employee from one country to their peers in another country for a week. Then COVID hit, so they had to cancel.

Since then, I have heard about other companies organizing this kind of Erasmus program. I think it's an excellent idea if you want your employees to discover another team's culture, gain new skills from their peers, and enhance communication, collaboration, and relationships. It can be done for a few days or longer, depending on your goals and capacity.

Companies' Erasmus programs might differ from job exchange programs, where people might swap positions and offices. What I like about initiatives such as the Team's Erasmus program is that you follow your peers and learn from them by participating in their daily work.

There are expenses associated with such an initiative, but the rewards make it worthwhile. Not only will the participating employees feel valued and learn from the experience, but they will also come back motivated with new ideas, a clear vision of the big picture, and feeling empowered by skill and knowledge transfer. In my opinion, this is a huge ROI for the team and the whole company. You can organize this kind of program between countries, offices, departments, or divisions. There are so many possibilities!

Having Fun – The Secret Ingredient for Relationships

Who enjoys a boring day in the office when everyone is behind their laptop, not speaking or socializing, and with the same facial expression the whole day? I don't.

Having fun, smiling, and laughing are part of my definition of happiness at work. Some of the best memories I have of my professional journey are related to having fun with my colleagues. We might have different needs and be at different levels, but let's face it, we spend so much time at work that we need to create a nice atmosphere.

I am not saying that work should become a comedy club all day, but like everything in life, having a good balance can benefit our well-being.

Numerous studies indicate that having fun at work can significantly boost employee engagement, creativity, and retention. When employees perceive their work environment as fun and supportive, their basic psychological needs are satisfied, which in turn fosters creativity and innovative thinking[3].

Sometimes, the simplest initiatives can be the best ones. From Secret Santa and theme days to office games, there are plenty of ways to have fun, but many factors might influence how people react to these initiatives. I've selected three other ideas for getting to know your colleagues on a deeper level with a fun twist:

IDEA 50

COFFEE BREAK FAVORITES

Tell me what's your favorite beverage, and I'll tell you who you are!

No, it's not that kind of quiz, but when ordering coffee for someone else there are so many specificities it can get complicated. Do you like your coffee with milk, without milk, with oat milk, with sugar, without sugar, or do you prefer tea or fresh fruit juice? Let's be honest; there are so many options that offering someone a coffee feels like navigating a beverage labyrinth!

Yet, when you randomly receive your drink of choice from a colleague, it will automatically make you smile!

This idea works great for smaller teams who share the same office space. Create a poster next to the coffee/tea machine featuring each team member's name and a funny picture, along with their favorite beverages.

The goal is to list everyone's drink preferences so you can surprise them with their favorite coffee, tea, or juice when they need a break! This little gesture amplifies kindness, creates opportunities to delight our colleagues, and fosters good relationships.

IDEA
51

FUN FACTS
ABOUT YOUR COLLEAGUES

Sometimes we think that we know our colleagues well until we ask them to share a fun fact about themselves!

What's one fun fact about you?

This question can be asked in different formats. It can work quite well as an icebreaker at the beginning of a meeting with new people, during a workshop, on a board in the office, or even in your newsletter/social media platform to announce new colleagues or spotlight an employee.

You might be surprised by what a colleague might share! I've heard facts like:

- *There is a farmer hidden in me; I have my own tractor*
- *I am a singer and rock the stage on Saturdays*
- *I volunteer for a women's community during my free time*
- *I wrote a novel two years ago*

A simple question can reveal unexpected and fascinating sides of your colleagues, helping to build stronger connections and a more positive workplace.

So go ahead—ask, share, and enjoy the surprises!

Scan the QR code to see a communication campaign in which a company shares fun facts about their employees.

IDEA 52

Here are the instructions for a fun team activity inspired by Management 3.0 to help colleagues get to know each other:

➡️ Ask each participant to take a flipchart or a large piece of paper (it's also possible to do it online with a virtual whiteboard). Have them draw a circle in the middle of the paper to write their name inside (optional).

➡️ Around the circle, they should write or draw anything they feel comfortable sharing about themselves: things related to family, hobbies, education, languages, favorite animals, favorite songs, goals, their definition of happiness at work (refer to Chapter 1), values, fun facts about themselves, strengths, and areas for improvement.

➡️ Once everyone has designed their personal maps, ask them to present someone else's map (don't tell them at first – that will be a fun twist). Presenting someone else's map allows people to ask more questions about what's on the board and show more interest than just listening. For an even more fun twist, people shouldn't write their names in the middle of the map, and the others have to guess whose map it is!

This team activity can be powerful and really fun to do to learn from each other. It can promote creativity, communication, empathy, and common interests among team members.

Beyond daily interactions, engaging in shared activities can deepen relationships and build a stronger sense of community within the team.

Doing Something Together to Build Bonds

Shared experiences create lasting connections. Whether it's a team lunch, a volunteer project, or a fun challenge, doing something together strengthens relationships, fosters collaboration, and enhances team spirit. These moments help build trust, improve communication, and create a sense of belonging—key ingredients for effective leadership and high-performing teams. I have selected three initiatives to inspire you to build bonds in different ways.

IDEA 53

MAKE YOUR TEAM EVENT IMPACTFUL

Let's be honest: Some team events or team-building activities can be overly simplistic and clichéd. Especially after a few years of experience, it can feel like you've done it all. However, the truth is that these activities are crucial and effective for enhancing collaboration, improving communication, and building strong bonds. Sometimes, the simplest activities can be the most enjoyable!

If you want to take your team event to the next level, consider replacing the usual outdoor activities, cooking classes, or escape rooms with an activity that can have a more meaningful and real impact on people or the environment.

Some examples I have seen:

➡ Planting trees to contribute towards a greener and more sustainable future.

➡ A recycling competition to reduce the amount of waste – on top, you can organize a DIY Workshop to learn how to turn plastic bottles and cartons into pieces of art.

➡ Cooking for homeless people in the area.

➡ Repainting an orphanage or children's center.

➡ Creating a garden corner on the office roof or in green areas.

- Participating as a team in a charity run or walk to raise money for a good cause.
- Giving language classes to refugees.

Engaging in acts of kindness and helping others can boost mood, enhance self-esteem, and foster meaningful social connections, all of which are crucial components of happiness.

IDEA 54

CHOOSE A TEAM CHALLENGE

Some people love to be challenged and compete, and some don't. Usually, team challenges are on a volunteering basis exactly for this reason. However, we often underestimate the effect of being part of a team challenge. It's not only fun, but it can develop our sense of belonging, trust, and team cohesion as we share the same goal. It can also help us manage conflict better, reduce stress, and enhance workplace dynamics.

Here are some ideas for team challenges that I find fun and powerful to encourage health and physical well-being:

- Take-the-stairs challenge to avoid taking elevators and allow your body to move more
- Track-your-steps challenge to avoid sitting too much at your desk
- Go to bed early or wake up early challenge – track your sleep
- Any sports challenge (yoga, running, bike to work, etc.)
- Meditation challenge to develop mindfulness
- Water-drinking challenge
- Plank challenge after a long meeting
- Book challenge

Whatever the team challenge, the goal is to do it with other people and motivate each other to complete or even win the challenge.

IDEA 55

We all have a story to share.

You have probably heard of TEDx, an organization based on voluntary work where the goal is to share ideas in speeches of less than 18 minutes on the famous red rounded carpet. The main goal of a TEDx speech is to spread ideas because, as their new motto explains very well: "Ideas Change Everything."

TEDx organizations are usually found in large cities. Anyone can submit their ideas, and if the committee team chooses your idea, you will have the opportunity to give your speech on stage. I did my TEDx in Zurich, Switzerland, during the pandemic on *"How to Be Truly Happy at Work."* What an experience! Watch it via the QR code at the end of the chapter.

TEDx also allows companies to host events. I have seen companies organizing an internal TEDx event for their employees. You can find more information on how to get a license on the official TEDx website.

I believe it's a fantastic idea to encourage employee participation voluntarily. You can create an organizational team and invite employees who would like to share an idea or a story. You can also have employees vote to select speakers. Perhaps there's a skilled public speaker among your employees who can coach future speakers. Involve employees in organizing the event; you can even encourage them to showcase their hidden talents, such as playing an instrument, singing, or dancing for entertainment in between the speeches as the real TEDx event does.

In the end, it's an event organized by the employees themselves. This kind of event with a common goal usually fosters bonds, a sense of belonging, and a shared challenge and vision.

The Power of Communities in Your Company

Being part of a community within the company can make a real difference at work. Many people feel lonely at work. We don't always get along with our team members, and with the rise of hybrid and remote work, we have fewer opportunities to meet new people. Building a sense of community within a company is essential to strengthen relationships, collaboration, inclusion, trust, and support, and avoid social isolation.

There are many ways to create communities in a company. You could base the community on:

- Nationality, language
- Common interests, hobbies, sports, or passions outside of work
- Knowledge sharing, training, and skill development
- Different backgrounds, cultures, and identities
- Well-being and social activities
- Charity work

Being part of a community at work creates a sense of belonging, allowing employees to connect over shared interests or goals, which boosts morale and encourages knowledge sharing and personal growth.

I am not going to go further into the above. What I will share for this section is the interesting story of Vanessa Gentile, Head of Marketing at Salesforce Switzerland.

She turned an internal community project into an independent European NGO.

IDEA 56

FROM AN INTERNAL COMMUNITY PROJECT TO A EUROPEAN NGO

Vanessa Gentile, Head of Marketing at Salesforce Switzerland, started an internal community within Salesforce in response to her manager's challenge to help attract more women talent in the technology sector. She leads us through the story behind turning a local community into a European NGO.

"

Everything started in my role as the Alliance and Channel Leader in Switzerland responsible for growing the Ecosystem with new Salesforce Certified people. The Ecosystem lacked talents, female talents. With a conversation I had with my partners I proposed to build a program to reskill female talents and increase the percentage of women in the Salesforce Ecosystem and in the technology sector. The partners were struggling to find those talents and they said, "We cannot find women for this position." I couldn't believe it! I argued that half the population is women, so there must be talented women out there for our company. We needed to change the situation and walk the talk, figure out how to attract women to our company and the technology sector. My partners nicely challenged me to find these women, and they promised to hire them. I had a mission, and I was determined to accomplish it.

This made me reflect on my own experiences. I was aware of the difficulties women face when returning to work after a career break – struggling with network access, visibility, and the need to reskill when their previous jobs no longer fit.

Growing up as a child of immigrant parents, I often felt like my presence wasn't valued. These experiences motivated me to create a platform to help others overcome educational barriers. After my second pregnancy, I found that my job had been given to someone else. Figuring out my next steps was a real challenge. I wished I had a mentor or coach to guide me through this tough time. Eventually, I decided to learn new skills in a different field. It was a difficult journey, as I had to learn everything on my own. I had to build my own network and establish myself as a leader in the workforce again.

My own experiences and the challenges I faced helped me create the initiative Bring Women Back to Work (BWBW) within my Alliance and Channel role at Salesforce Switzerland. I was convinced that education is a fundamental right, and the mission of BWBW would be to offer free, accessible, and high-quality educational resources to women to equip them with knowledge, networks, and the right personal support, such as mentorship and coaching.

With such a community of women talents, I thought that companies like the Salesforce Ecosystem would be able to find talented women more easily.

Starting with a handful of committed volunteers from Salesforce who embraced my vision, we launched local online workshops, classes, and events to emphasize the importance of education and provide direct learner support. The initiative quickly gained momentum, and our community expanded outside the Ecosystem. A significant milestone for BWBW was the introduction of our 12-month online program, which broadened our reach and allowed us to deliver educational content to a wider audience, thanks to all the content partners who volunteered to support the cause. Our platform evolved into a learning and networking hub, offering a variety of resources, including video tutorials, interactive courses, and comprehensive online mentorship and coaching. With such a support and training platform, these women who had a career gap or were in transition could learn new skills such as technical skills, social competencies, and human skills, and they even learned more about mental health. They were better equipped to be hired by our partners, who were part of our pool of hiring companies.

As BWBW significantly grew, we transformed it from a community into an independent NGO developed in different countries. It continues to evolve, respecting our initial principles of inclusivity, accessibility, and community empowerment. Our future plans include developing specialized programs for marginalized groups, expanding our language options, and collaborating with local organizations to ensure our resources are culturally relevant and impactful. Furthermore, most of our alumni stay within the community supporting as mentors after graduation to give back to the community, which is how we grow and support each other. Other alumni become independent as coaches and are delivering services like content workshops for free.

— Vanessa Gentile, Head of Marketing, Salesforce Switzerland

Vanessa's story highlights the power of communities to enhance relationships at work and the importance of promoting volunteer work within a company. Volunteering on a meaningful project can significantly boost one's happiness, sense of belonging, and purpose.

Salesforce provides each employee 56 hours of paid volunteer time off each year, which allows employees to participate in impactful projects.

They are the founder and champion of Pledge 1%, a global movement to ensure giving back is part of companies of all sizes.

The company demonstrates its commitment to philanthropy through its 1-1-1 model, dedicating 1% of its equity, product, and employee time to community service. The goal is to inspire, educate, and empower all businesses to leverage their assets and make social impact an integral part of their company.

As Vanessa shared with me, they are fostering the syndrome of giving back within the company! A true inspiration for the employees.

Since 2014, more than 18,000 companies in over 100 countries have joined the Pledge 1% movement. Scan the QR code to get more info.

DEI for Building Strong Workplace Relationships

One of the benefits of Diversity, Equity, and Inclusion (DEI) initiatives is their ability to foster understanding between groups and build stronger workplace relationships. While DEI is a topic worthy of its own book, I won't delve into its broader aspects here. Instead, my goal in this chapter is to highlight a fascinating DEI initiative that has significantly enhanced workplace relationships.

IDEA 57

CULTURAL VILLAGE
TO PROMOTE DEI

Company Spotlight – PMI – by Maxime Magnier

Maxime Magnier, Manager Business Engagement at Philip Morris International (PMI), collaborated with his colleagues to establish a Cultural Village with the aim of highlighting the diverse cultures and nationalities within the company. Their first event took place at the Research and Development Center in Neuchatel, Switzerland, and following its success, they adapted the concept for the headquarters office in Lausanne. Both events helped the employees to connect with their colleagues and develop deep relationships at work.

Maxime guides us through the entire process of organizing the events, the challenges they faced, and the outcomes:

In 2023, we established a local volunteer employee action group to promote diversity, equity, and inclusion (DEI) and a sense of belonging within the company. One of the ideas from two group ambassadors, Anthony and Susan, was to organize a Cultural Village event to develop more connections, break down silos, highlight the diversity of our employees, and promote exchange among us all. They wanted everyone to travel around the world and discover their colleagues' cultures without even leaving the office.

The concept was simple: We would set up a table, a screen, and a whiteboard to allow people to share their culture through traditional food, images, music, traditional costumes, pictures, decorations, and specific objects from their own homes. We had a two-hour slot during lunchtime, and we planned to use a common area for everyone to view the event.

We initially put out a "call for volunteers" to find individuals interested in representing their countries as ambassadors during our cultural village event. We received an amazing response with 22 countries being represented. Some

NURTURING MEANINGFUL WORKPLACE RELATIONSHIPS 139

booths had four or more people representing their respective countries. Everyone was very enthusiastic about the idea and showed great creativity. They were responsible for preparing their traditional dishes and organizing their booth. The cooking aspect presented a challenge as we needed special permission for safety reasons. For our future events, we are considering collaborating directly with our local canteen so that participants can cook on-site with our staff.

The outcome has been above our expectations. Many employees learned about different cultures and became extremely curious. The food element helped break barriers, allowing us to connect and share our stories regardless of age, gender, or culture. Many employees formed new connections, and some even discovered that they share the same nationalities with colleagues they didn't know about before. The event simultaneously highlighted diversity, inclusion, exchange, a sense of belonging, and curiosity.

It was an event organized by the employees for the employees – that was the magic behind it!

Based on this first success, we adapted the concept for our headquarters office in Lausanne in Spring 2024. In the second event, they even organized a quiz for the booth visitors. Adding a gaming element created even more fun and discussion.

Building on the success and how people are enjoying and talking about the positive cultural impact of the event from Neuchatel, one employee (Mathilde) decided to collect all recipes from all countries represented in the booths. Then, we created an internal cookbook, printed copies ourselves, and sold them within the company to collect money for our internal association platform (Project With Heart). We sold more than 200 books after the event, and people are now asking to do this event every year!

– Maxime Magnier, Manager Business Engagement, PMI

Maxime's approach highlights the magic of employee-driven events that foster connection and understanding. This reminds me of the saying, *"The way to someone's heart is through their stomach."* Food is a great bridge between cultures and a wonderful way to create new bonds.

Strong relationships are the foundation of a positive work culture and are built over time. Strengthening those bonds will create a more supportive, productive, and joyful workplace for teams. Building strong workplace relationships also relies on understanding and valuing the emotions and perspectives of others. In the next chapter, we'll explore how cultivating emotional intelligence can enhance our connections, allowing us to communicate with empathy, manage conflicts effectively, and foster a truly collaborative environment.

CHAPTER HIGHLIGHTS

✔

A human-centric culture is fostered by strong workplace relationships.

✔

Fun and culture-appropriate team-building initiatives can help
build a sense of togetherness in your organization.

✔

Building a sense of community within a company is essential
to strengthen relationships, collaboration, inclusion, trust,
support, and avoid social isolation.

✔

Meaningful conversations with emotional connection
build healthy and genuine connections.

✔

It is important to respect the emotional boundaries of others.

✔

Meetings don't have to always be by the book – switch things up with walk
and talks, online meetings, and personalized meetings!

LET'S TAKE ACTION

As you reflect on the importance of relationships at work, consider the steps you can take to nurture a more connected and collaborative environment.

➡️ **Start Small:** Choose one initiative from this chapter and try it out with your team this week. Notice the difference it makes in how you interact and collaborate. Which initiative will you try first?

➡️ **Stay Consistent:** Building strong relationships takes time and effort. Commit to regularly incorporating these practices into your work routine to maintain and grow the bonds within your team.

➡️ **Encourage your team members** to share their own experiences and ideas for fostering connections. Together, you can create a workplace culture that values and prioritizes human connection.

Access additional resources by scanning the QR code.

YOUR THOUGHTS
YOUR JOURNEY

Capture your insights, ideas, and action steps as you make this journey your own.

6

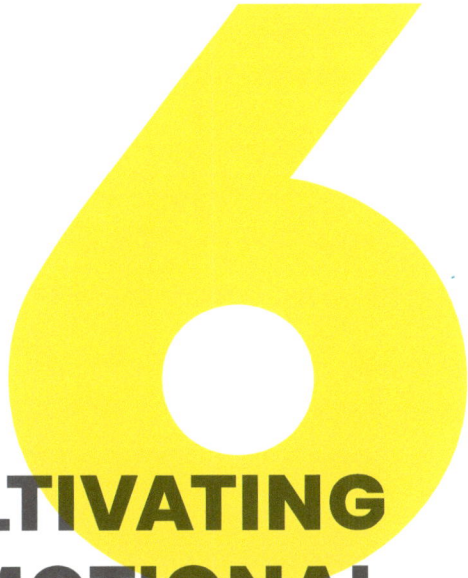

CULTIVATING EMOTIONAL INTELLIGENCE AT WORK

Your EI
Will Make the Difference

Emotional Intelligence (EI) is the ability to understand, manage, and use your own emotions effectively while recognizing and responding to the emotions of those around you. EQ (Emotional Quotient) is often used interchangeably with EI, but EQ specifically refers to the measurable aspect of Emotional Intelligence—whereas EI represents the skillset itself.

EI is a set of skills that can be learned and developed over time. It allows us to understand ourselves better, maintain positive relationships, and cope with major challenges in effective ways. Essentially, it's about how you manage yourself and your relationships with others.

Emotional Intelligence is key to workplace success because it enhances the ability to navigate complex social interactions, manage stress, and make balanced decisions. Leaders with high EI foster better team cohesion and create an environment where employees feel understood and valued, leading to higher morale, engagement, and productivity.

Although EI and EQ are not new concepts, they have long been overshadowed by the omnipresent IQ (Intelligence Quotient). Today, emotional intelligence has gained significant attention due to shifts in our way of working and how we approach leadership. Human skills such as empathy, problem-solving, and active listening now play a crucial role in the workplace. While technical skills remain important, especially with the rise of artificial intelligence (AI), this technology has limitations—unlike humans, it cannot truly understand or experience emotions. As automation increases, so does the demand for meaningful and authentic human interactions. This highlights the importance of mastering the human skills that technology cannot replace.

Your IQ is not enough anymore
your EQ will make the difference.

In our evolving workplace, shaped by hybrid models, remote work, and digital communication, social skills have become more critical than ever. The study "Emotional Intelligence and Job Performance: A Meta-Analysis" by Jaroslaw Grobelny, Patrycja Radke, and Daria Paniotova, published in the International Journal of Work Organization and Emotion (2021), investigates the relationship between emotional intelligence and job performance. This comprehensive study reviewed 99 other studies with a total sample size of 17,889 participants, making it one of the largest meta-analyses on this topic. The results showed that EI has a significant positive correlation with job performance[1].

Employees with higher
Emotional Intelligence
perform better at work.

There are similar results for job satisfaction and engagement at work. Another meta-analysis by Miao, Humphrey, and Qian (2017)[2] explores the relationship between emotional intelligence and work-related attitudes like job satisfaction and organizational commitment. Employees with higher EI tend to be more satisfied and more engaged in their work.

Daniel Goleman, American psychologist, author, and science journalist, popularized the concept of emotional intelligence with his bestseller books on the topic. Let's explore his expertise:

With Daniel Goleman

Daniel Goleman, renowned American psychologist and expert in emotional intelligence, emphasizes that:

➡ Emotional intelligence refers to a different way of being smart.
➡ EI is key to high performance, particularly for outstanding leadership. It's not about your IQ but how you manage yourself and your relationship with others.
➡ Being an emotionally intelligent leader can pay dividends when it comes to inspiring teams, managing stress, staying focused, delivering feedback, empathizing with colleagues, and working together.

The four domains Daniel Goleman focuses on in his leadership model of emotional intelligence are:

➡ **Self-awareness:** The ability to recognize and understand your own emotions and how they affect your behavior and performance.
➡ **Self-management:** The ability to manage and control your own emotions, impulses, and resources in healthy ways, which includes staying calm under pressure and maintaining integrity.
➡ **Social awareness:** The ability to understand and empathize with others' emotions, often referred to as empathy, and to read the emotional currents in an organization or group.
➡ **Relationship management:** The ability to manage and influence relationships, including skills such as communication, teamwork, conflict resolution, and inspiring others.

Sources: Daniel Goleman, bestselling author of many books on Emotional Intelligence[3].

This topic is vast and could be developed much more. However, I'll briefly describe the main domains of Emotional Intelligence based on the Daniel Goleman model, so you can understand what it means and how you can develop those skills with hands-on tools and techniques.

Self-Awareness: The First Step to Develop Your EI

Self-awareness is the cornerstone of emotional intelligence. It involves recognizing your own emotions, strengths, personality, and behaviors, and understanding how they impact both yourself and others. By being more in tune with your emotional state, you can improve your ability to manage your reactions, make well-informed decisions, and cultivate healthier relationships.

Emotions can serve as signals, and they can vary depending on the situation. They can even be contradictory; for example, you can feel happy and stressed at the same time. Reflecting on your emotional responses in different situations and trying to identify the triggers behind them will help you gain deeper insights into your thoughts and feelings.

IDEA 58

5 WAYS TO SELF-ASSESS YOUR FEELINGS

In order to develop self-awareness, practice regularly checking in with yourself.

Here are five ways you can choose to self-assess your feelings:

1. Journaling every day to reflect on your daily emotions, situations that trigger your emotions, and how you respond to them.
2. Mindfulness meditation and focusing on your breathing can help you gain awareness and clarity about your emotions.
3. Focus on the moment to pay attention to your thoughts and emotions: Pause to assess your feelings. Ask yourself: *"How am I feeling right now?"* – The more you check in, the more self-aware you'll become.
4. Reflect on your day and experiences with compassion. Don't be too self-critical; be gentle with yourself, as you would be with your best friend.

5. Ask for constructive feedback to assess your behaviors and emotions perceived by others. Ask them, for example, what they notice about your tendencies and triggers.

Also, pay attention to the physical reactions that come with your emotions, such as a tight chest, sweaty palms, and a fast heartbeat. The body responds to emotions in defined ways. Being aware of your body's signals can assist you in identifying the emotion you are feeling.

It's important to acknowledge your emotions without judgment, whether positive or negative. When we acknowledge challenging emotions, we get through them with less intensity. Conversely, if emotions are pushed aside or ignored, they tend to grow stronger.

Setting intentions for yourself is also a powerful tool. Visualizing how you want your day to be and how you want to feel will enhance your self-awareness.

IDEA 59

ADD YOUR TO-BE TO YOUR TO-DO LIST

The concept of "adding your to-be to your to-do" emphasizes the importance of aligning your daily tasks with the qualities or values you want to embody. This goes beyond merely focusing on task completion – it's about *who* you are while doing those tasks or *how* you perform the task.

Traditional to-do lists often outline tasks based on external demands and goals, such as meeting deadlines or completing specific tasks. The idea behind having a to-be list is to remind ourselves of the qualities we want to embody, such as being more patient, empathetic, or creative, alongside our tasks.

For example, while your to-do list might include "finish a report," your to-be list might show "be collaborative" or "stay calm under pressure."

Or if you are having your 1:1 sessions with your team members, your to-be might reflect "show empathy" or "offer support."

ADD "TO-BE" TO YOUR "TO-DO"

By consciously incorporating these qualities into your actions, you make a connection between your personal growth and your tasks, leading to a more intentional and fulfilling day. It's a powerful way to ensure that your daily actions not only accomplish tasks but also help you become the person you aspire to be.

Being aware and visualizing how we want to feel helps us switch from only "doing" to "being"!

We own our emotions; they don't own us!

Understanding your emotions is only part of the equation. The next key element is self-management, which empowers you to regulate these emotions and respond constructively. Let's explore how to manage your emotions for a healthier, more productive work experience.

Self-Management: Learn to Regulate Your Emotions

You are not your emotions! While emotions are a natural part of being human, they don't define you. Instead, they serve as valuable information, signaling how a situation affects you. The key to emotional intelligence is learning to put space between your emotions and your reactions.

**You may not always be able
to control how you feel,
but you can choose how
to respond to your emotions.**

When a strong emotion arises, it's easy to react impulsively. But by pausing and observing the emotion, you can identify what you're feeling without being overwhelmed by it.

Ask yourself, *"What is this emotion telling me?"*

Then, take a moment to decide how you want to respond, rather than letting the emotion dictate your behavior.

This ability to pause, reflect, and choose your reaction helps you take control of your behavior, leading to more thoughtful and constructive outcomes. By practicing this regularly, you build greater emotional resilience, self-awareness, and self-management, which empowers you to navigate your emotions with clarity and purpose.

A powerful technique to manage and regulate your emotions is using breathing techniques to calm down and unwind.

IDEA 60
MASTER EMOTIONAL REGULATION WITH THE 4-7-8 TECHNIQUE

The 4-7-8 breathing technique is an effective method for developing emotional self-regulation. This technique helps to calm the nervous system and can be particularly useful when dealing with anxiety or strong emotions.

Here's how to practice the 4-7-8 breathing technique:

➡ Inhale through your nose for a count of **4**.

➡ Hold your breath for a count of **7**.

➡️ Exhale slowly and completely through your mouth for a count of **8**, making a whooshing sound.

By focusing on your breath, you create a pause between feeling an emotion and reacting to it, which gives you time to choose a more measured response.

Regular practice of the 4-7-8 breathing technique strengthens emotional resilience and enhances your ability to respond thoughtfully to challenging emotions. Scan the QR code to access a guided 4-7-8 breathing exercise. I will introduce box breathing, another breathing technique, in Chapter 9 on Stress Management.

Learning to manage your emotions will help bring your brain back to mental clarity and cultivate a positive mindset. You'll recognize that you have a choice in how you respond to your emotions.

Other mindfulness techniques, such as meditation, journaling, and mindful walking, help quiet the mind and allow you to ground yourself in the present moment. This helps cultivate greater emotional balance and self-regulation. Additionally, the techniques in Chapter 9, such as staying focused and managing stress levels, will also help manage your emotions.

Taking the time for self-reflection, being aware of emotions, and learning how to manage them is the foundation of emotional intelligence. It will help identify stress before it becomes overwhelming and too difficult to manage.

Understanding the reasons behind your emotions and reactions provides valuable insights. By recognizing triggers, controlling negative impulses, and directing emotions in a constructive manner, you can develop emotional intelligence. This skill requires ongoing practice, but the benefits make it worth the effort.

Our social skills help us navigate social interactions, communicate effectively, and collaborate with others. Social skills are the practical application of emotional intelligence.

Now that we've explored how to manage our own emotions, the next crucial step is social awareness – understanding and responding to the emotions of others. This is essential for effective teamwork and collaboration.

Social Awareness:
Understand the Emotions of Others

Social awareness is a critical component of emotional intelligence as it involves the ability to recognize and understand the emotions of others. It enables individuals to effectively engage with others, encouraging collaboration and improving team dynamics. Social awareness plays a vital role in leadership, teamwork, and creating a supportive organizational culture.

Understanding other people's emotions and seeing things from their perspective is another critical emotional intelligence skill: it's called empathy.

IDEA 61

10 IMPACTFUL PHRASES TO FOSTER EMPATHY AT WORK

Empathy competence involves being able to understand and resonate with others' emotions and seeing things from their perspectives, as well as showing genuine interest in their concerns and problems.

When we ask our colleagues or team members, *"How are you?"* it might be a genuine question indeed, but it can be difficult for them to answer anything other than *"I'm fine!"* Depending on their situation, they might feel differently. To show more empathy, we can ask specific questions that will help the person feel heard and be more detailed with their response. This can lead to more authentic, deeper, and more honest discussions.

One way to increase empathy when talking to other people is to recognize that their feelings are valid.

Here are four questions to help develop empathy in teams:

○ *What mix of feelings do you have right now?*
This question opens the space for sharing multiple emotions, developing the discussion, and understanding the need beneath the feelings. Feelings are messages that might explain something deeper than what's on the surface.

○ **What challenges are you currently facing, and how can I or the team support you?**
This invites openness and shows that you care about their well-being and are willing to help.

○ **Is there anything happening outside of work affecting your focus or energy that you'd like to share?**
This question allows team members to express more personal challenges that might be influencing their work, helping you support them holistically.

○ **What can we do as a team to create a more supportive and understanding work environment?**
This promotes collective empathy and invites suggestions for improving the team's emotional culture.

Here are two other kinds of questions that are more focused on self-reflection to develop your own empathy:

○ **How would I feel in their situation?**
Consider their perspective and emotions by imagining yourself in their shoes. This builds deeper emotional understanding.

○ **How can I validate their feelings, even if I don't fully agree with their viewpoint?**
Empathy is about acknowledging someone's emotions without judgment. This question guides you toward offering supportive, non-defensive responses. Feeling connected with your own emotions and being empathetic toward yourself will make you more effective in showing empathy in a conversation. Having empathy toward yourself will help you to grow and have more compassion.

Now, let's analyze four sentences to demonstrate empathy in a conversation:

○ **I can see this situation is really tough for you, and I'm here to listen and support you however you need.**
Acknowledging someone's struggle and offering support demonstrates empathy and helps build trust, making the person feel understood and less isolated.

- *I understand this must be frustrating for you. Let's see how we can work through it together.*

  Expressing understanding of frustration and proposing to work together promotes collaboration and reassures the person that they are not facing the challenge alone.

- *I completely get why you feel that way; your concerns are valid, and we can find a solution.*

  Validating concerns and showing a willingness to find solutions strengthens mutual respect and encourages constructive problem-solving.

- *It sounds like you've been through a lot lately – thank you for sharing that with me.*

  Recognizing someone's emotional experiences and thanking them for sharing builds rapport and trust, and creates a safe space for open communication.

Empathy is about creating an emotional connection, a shared space to feel connected with others. The questions or sentences we use in a conversation will either build bridges of understanding or widen the gap between us. By choosing our words thoughtfully, we invite openness and trust, fostering a culture where people feel valued, heard, and supported. In the end, empathy is not just a skill but a practice that transforms the way we relate to one another, creating stronger, more positive relationships in the workplace.

IDEA 62

5 WAYS TO PAY ATTENTION TO OTHERS

Developing social awareness in teams involves understanding and being attentive to the emotions, needs, and dynamics of others. It's about recognizing verbal and nonverbal cues and adjusting your actions accordingly. There are different ways to start paying attention to others and develop social awareness:

1. **Pay attention to their body language**

    Body language says a lot about how someone really feels. Watch for positive signs that show they're receptive, such as eye contact, relaxed posture, smiling, and nodding. On the other end, negative body language, even if unconsciously given, can signal resistance, dishonesty, or discomfort and can affect communication, trust, and team dynamics. Common negative cues are crossed arms, tone of voice, finger or foot tapping, legs crossed, or frowning. Take notice of nonverbal communication, body language, and even the vocabulary they use to get a conversation going.

2. Ask open-ended questions in a conversation

Using open-ended inquiries can be a successful method for encouraging others to engage in conversation. It shows you're engaged and want to get to know them better. Instead of the typical *"How are you?"* or *"Did you have a good weekend?"* try *"How do you feel about …?"* *"What do you think of …?"* or *"What did you get up to this weekend?"* Colleagues might welcome open-ended questions better because it demonstrates your interest in their thoughts.

3. Observe and connect on the emotional level first

Instead of jumping into work-related topics immediately, ensure you observe the room, be aware of the overall vibe, and connect on an emotional level first. Ask questions to assess the other person's state of mind. This will give you better awareness about how this person feels and provide an excellent opportunity for them to self-reflect and develop their own self-awareness. For example, apply the "2-word check-in" explained in Chapter 5. Depending on the response, you can adapt the conversation, your tone, or your behaviors.

The same applies to groups. When starting a team meeting, it's always helpful to "take the pulse of the room" by observing and asking about their energy level or how they feel today. It gives the presenter the proper social awareness to adapt their energy level, communication, or even the content.

4. See the world through other people's eyes

Develop your empathy skills. Try to walk in their shoes for a moment and understand what it is like to be them or feel what they feel. Refer to the ten impactful sentences previously explained in this chapter.

5. Tune into your own emotions

Remember that before you can understand others, it's important to be aware of your own emotions. Our brains are wired with mirror neurons (discussed in more detail in Chapter 9), which help us sense and reflect the emotions of those around us. These neurons are part of what enables us to empathize.

Take a moment to check in with yourself: *"How does this situation make me feel?"* By becoming aware of your own feelings, you'll be better equipped to pick up on the emotional signals others are sending and navigate better emotional dynamics in the workplace.

Being socially aware involves being in tune with the general mood or ambiance of a social setting. Adapting your actions based on this mood can help you interact more effectively. Once you've assessed the overall atmosphere, you can modify your behavior to align with it or respond appropriately to whatever atmosphere is present. With experience, interpreting the emotional atmosphere in social contexts will become intuitive.

Relationship Management: Managing Social Interactions Successfully

Relationship management, as defined by Daniel Goleman in the context of emotional intelligence, involves the ability to build and maintain healthy, productive relationships with others. This domain focuses on effectively managing interactions, resolving conflicts, and inspiring and influencing those around you.

To help you improve this skill, I will showcase some techniques to adapt your listening behaviors, communicate with emotional intelligence effectively, and manage conflict in the context of the workplace.

IDEA 63

Mastering the art of listening can be a challenge, but it's crucial for effective communication. Good listening encourages open communication, builds trust, strengthens relationships, and promotes a more collaborative and empathetic environment.

When listening, paying attention to your behaviors is essential, as they communicate your level of engagement and respect. Your behaviors during a conversation shape how others feel heard and understood, enhancing trust and the quality of the interaction.

Follow this simple acronym to become a better listener.

LEARN TO LISTEN

	L	LEAVE DISTRACTIONS
	I	INTENTION
	S	SILENCE
	T	TELL ME MORE
	E	EMPATHY
	N	NONVERBAL COMMUNICATION

L – Leave distractions behind

In any conversation, it's vital to remove distractions like your phone, emails, or other interruptions. By setting these aside, you signal to the other person that they have your full attention, fostering a more focused and meaningful exchange.

I – Clarify the Intention

Define the purpose of the discussion and your intention. Are you listening to provide feedback, allow the other person to vent, or offer a solution? Understanding your role helps guide the conversation in a productive direction and ensures the person feels supported.

S – Silence is key

Instead of jumping into the conversation with your own thoughts, let the other person speak without interrupting. Silence creates space for them to fully express their story, thoughts, or emotions, helping them feel heard. It also gives you time to process what they're saying and respond thoughtfully.

T – Tell me more

Encourage deeper conversation by prompting the other person to elaborate. Paraphrase their message, use phrases like *"Tell me more," "What do you mean by that?"* or *"Could you give me a specific example?"* or ask follow-up questions, which show genuine interest and help uncover important details, fostering better understanding.

E – Show Empathy

Demonstrate understanding and compassion for the person's feelings and experiences. Empathy allows you to connect emotionally, creating a supportive and trusting environment where the speaker feels safe to share.

N – Nonverbal communication matters

Your body language, facial expressions, and overall attitude play a big role in how your listening is perceived. Maintain eye contact, nod, and avoid crossing your arms, as these nonverbal cues convey openness and engagement, reinforcing your attention to the conversation.

Remember these actionable tips to enhance your listening skills and behaviors.

A conversation is an exchange that has the potential to shape perceptions, emotions, and outcomes. The words we choose and the way we structure our sentences have a profound impact on how our message is received. A slight shift in phrasing can turn a neutral statement into an empowering one, or vice versa. Every word carries weight, and when chosen thoughtfully, they can inspire, motivate, and foster understanding. On the other hand, poorly chosen words can lead to misunderstanding or conflict. By being intentional with our language, we maximize the positive impact of our communication.

IDEA 64

10 POWERFUL PHRASES USED BY EI LEADERS

Incorporating emotionally intelligent language into our daily conversations can transform how we connect with others, whether we lead a team or not. Each of us can benefit from incorporating this language into our daily interactions to create a more empathetic and supportive environment for everyone around us.

These simple yet powerful phrases can build trust, encourage collaboration, and foster team growth:

○ *I hear you, and I understand your perspective.*
Acknowledging the feelings and viewpoints of others builds trust and openness.

○ *How can I support you in achieving this?*
Emotionally intelligent leaders focus on empowering others and offering support to help them grow = we are a team.

○ *What do you think?*
Encouraging team members to share their insights, promoting inclusivity and valuing diverse opinions.

○ *How could we make this better?*
Showing that you're open to ideas and input and that collaboration will help everyone to achieve the best results.

○ *Sorry, my fault!*

No one is perfect – we all fail or make mistakes – we are human! By owning your mistakes, you build trust.

○ *What have we learned from this that we can use next time?*

Avoid blaming. Everyone can learn from what happened and improve for next time. It's more important to learn how mistakes can be avoided than to allocate blame.

○ *We're in this together; let's find a solution as a team.*

Reinforcing collaboration and shared ownership in overcoming challenges boosts team cohesion.

○ *Do you have the capacity to do this?*

Managing extra workload and priorities and teaching employees to say no. It also acts to remind them that as an emotionally intelligent leader, you are interested in their health as part of their well-being and their success.

○ *How are you feeling about this?*

Inviting emotional check-ins helps to create emotional awareness and open dialogue within teams.

○ *Thank you, you've done a great job!*

Giving recognition, praise, and positive feedback has no cost!

What gets recognized, gets repeated, and you want to encourage your people to repeat good performance. It's simple, yet massively impactful.

Start integrating these phrases and notice their impact on your relationships and team dynamics.

While developing empathy allows us to understand the emotions and perspectives of others better, it's only one part of fostering a harmonious work environment. Effective conflict management builds on this foundation by addressing differences constructively, ensuring that empathy leads not just to understanding but also to resolution and growth. Let's explore how managing conflict effectively can transform workplace dynamics and strengthen team collaboration.

IDEA 65

SKIP WORKPLACE DRAMA WITH CONFLICT MANAGEMENT

Managing conflict effectively is not about forcing your own opinion on others or choosing a side. It means having the ability to navigate emotional or tense situations, understanding and recognizing different perspectives, handling disagreements tactfully, and finding common ground that everyone can endorse.

Conflict in the workplace can arise due to misunderstandings, lack of communication, lack of teamwork, poor leadership, workplace stress, and so on. Even in the most harmonious relationships, some level of disagreement is inevitable as individuals have different perspectives.

Conflict can negatively impact employees and the business. Employees might experience stress, lack of motivation, frustration, anxiety, and a decrease in self-esteem. The organization may witness reduced productivity, low employee morale, higher employee turnover, and potential customer service challenges, among other issues. On the flip side, if well managed, conflict can also promote growth, creativity, learning, and personal development. It can open up communication and develop new perspectives.

Here are tools you can use if you find yourself in a conflict:

- **Regulate your emotions first:** Emotional reactions can escalate conflict. Being too emotional in a discussion will not help address the conflict effectively. It's important to be calm and balanced before addressing the issue.
- **Choose the right time and place:** While it's important to address the issue early, it's also important to give both parties some time to cool down. Some conflicts might be better addressed privately in a neutral and private setting.
- **Turn "You" Into "I":** as we will address in Chapter 8 about feedback, using the "I" statement will help to focus on how the situation made you feel and the impact it had on you rather than blaming the other person.

For example, say, *"I felt frustrated," "I didn't understand," "I felt let down," "I felt humiliated when…"* etc. instead of starting with *"You [+ blame]."*

- **Listen actively, show empathy, and be open to other's perspective:** It will show respect and help you understand the other person's point of view. To emphasize this point, paraphrase and use the L-I-S-T-E-N tip and empathy sentences previously explained in this chapter. Understand their side.

- **Stay focused on the issue and not the person:** Keep the conversation centered on the specific conflict and avoid personal attacks or criticism. Remember that you both have a shared problem you need to solve together.

- **Acknowledge the other's opinion:** You might hear critical feedback about your work or behavior during the conversation. Reflect on what has been said (even if it's not easy to hear), acknowledge that you might be part of the problem, and identify areas to improve.

- **Find common ground:** Collaborate on a solution that addresses both parties' needs and where both feel heard and respected. If needed, seek support from a neutral third party to manage the conversation.

Having a neutral party to manage conflicts can be beneficial. This mediator can listen to all sides involved and help find common ground. This role is typically taken on by a leader, but it can also be an employee managing a conflict between two colleagues.

The neutral third person will have to create a safe space for dialogue and pay attention to certain factors in the conversation:

- **Clearly define expectations and boundaries:** Establish rules such as no interruptions, yelling, or aggressive behavior. Emphasize the importance of respect and acceptable behavior to reach a mutually beneficial solution.

- **Recognize and acknowledge the conflict:** Validate the feelings of both parties and rephrase their concerns to show understanding and respect.

- **Start by identifying common ground**: Encourage the parties to recognize areas of agreement before addressing their differences.

- **Pay attention to nonverbal cues:** Be aware of signs of disagreement, tension, or dissatisfaction. Your social awareness and skills are essential in this context.

- **Identify resistances and triggers:** Find out what led to the conflict if necessary. It should be relevant to the specific situation.
- **Monitor your own emotions:** As a third party, you might be in front of someone crying or angry. Keep your emotions balanced and stay calm so that you can listen actively, think straight, show empathy, and respond accordingly.

If the conversation does not lead to a practical solution or improvement, consider taking a break and revisiting the discussion later. Follow up on the conversation and try again if necessary.

Emotional intelligence is not just a personal asset; it's also a powerful tool for fostering positive relationships, enhancing decision-making, and creating a thriving work culture. It is essential to provide consistent training for employees and leaders to enhance their social skills and learn to transition from being managers or bosses to becoming true coaches and mentors. This shift creates an environment of growth, trust, and collaboration.

It is essential to recognize that our motivation and actions impact the four domains of emotional intelligence. By prioritizing emotional intelligence, companies can create a culture that promotes innovation, resilience, and meaningful leadership.

Remember:

Developing emotional intelligence takes time and practice. It's a work in progress because we are all human.

Depending on the day and situation, we might be better or worse at applying our emotional intelligence. If we try to develop these skills and incorporate the strategies explained in this chapter into our daily lives, we can significantly improve our relationships and social skills step by step, and become more effective team members.

In the following chapter, we'll see how these skills are essential for authentic and positive leadership, empowering leaders to inspire trust, resilience, and motivation within their teams.

CHAPTER HIGHLIGHTS

✔

Emotional intelligence is the ability to understand and manage your own emotions and those of the people around you.

✔

In our contemporary work setting, developing social skills is a must.

✔

It's important to acknowledge your emotions without judgment, whether they are positive or negative. When we acknowledge challenging emotions, we get through them with less intensity.

✔

You may not always be able to control how you feel, but you can choose how to respond to your emotions.

✔

Understanding other people's emotions and seeing things from their perspective is another critical emotional intelligence skill: it's called empathy.

✔

Use your EI skills to manage conflict effectively.

LET'S TAKE ACTION

➡️ Which emotional intelligence domains are you the strongest in?
Self-Awareness / Self-Management / Social Awareness or Relationship
Management.
Analyze what you are doing to develop it:

➡️ Which domains should you definitely improve?
What can you implement to improve it? Be specific in your response:

➡️ Select three sentences (from the lists in this chapter) to show more
empathy and develop EI at work and apply it within your team.
Observe how you feel saying it and observe the reaction of the receiver.

Access additional resources by scanning the QR code.

YOUR THOUGHTS
YOUR JOURNEY

Capture your insights, ideas, and action steps as you make this journey your own.

7

LEADING WITH AUTHENTICITY AND POSITIVITY

The Power
of Positive Leadership

Positivity isn't just a personality trait; it's a skill that can be developed and continuously improved.

When I work with leadership teams, I often hear:

- *We always need to be at the top of our game*
- *I feel lonely at the top*
- *I can't always share my struggles and challenges*

Being a leader is not always easy.

Despite the challenges and obstacles that leaders face, learning to lead authentically and positively is essential. While you may share the same fears and challenges as others, it's crucial not to let them control your actions. Nobody wants to follow someone who is negative all the time or cannot effectively manage their stress level. In fact, positive leadership has a significant impact on the workplace.

Leaders have an influence on the well-being and mental health of their teams. Although, as we said earlier, they are not responsible for employees' happiness, their actions and behaviors can significantly influence it.

Therefore, it is essential to be mindful of your emotions, behaviors, and the culture you are creating within your team. Your attitude and leadership style have a profound impact on your team's mental health, happiness, and performance. Again, I am not saying that we should always be positive or fake positivity, but let's admit that it's hard to motivate and inspire others if you have a negative attitude.

Top reasons for losing talents:
Poor leadership and poor work culture.

As discussed in Chapter 3, on Well-being, a meta-analysis of almost 94,000 employees[1] has shown that those who work under destructive leaders often experience worse objective mental health outcomes (stress, anxiety, burnout, absenteeism). On the other hand, employees who work with leaders who cultivate a vision, consider people's needs, and invest in building positive relationships tend to report more positive mental health outcomes (job satisfaction, high engagement rate, psychological well-being, creativity).

Therefore, it is crucial to understand that your leadership style strongly influences the work culture and mental health of your employees.

IDEA 66

UNDERSTAND YOUR LEADERSHIP STYLE

Understanding your leadership style is critical. It helps you see how your behaviors and actions impact those around you while also highlighting your strengths and areas for development.

Which style resonates most with you?

- **Transformational:** Motivates and inspires change and growth
- **Delegative:** Grants autonomy and trust
- **Autocratic:** Directs, controls and focuses on results
- **Transactional:** Focuses on achieving goals through rewards and incentives
- **Participative:** Engages in decision-making
- **Servant:** Prioritizes team development and well-being
- **Coaching:** Focuses on feedback and individual growth

Do you think that your current leadership style is effective?

There are many different ways to evaluate your leadership style. You can determine it based on the previously listed styles, a personality test, and/or your strengths. Scan the QR code to access personality test examples and more resources.

Keep in mind that no one leadership style is appropriate for all situations. You might use a different leadership style depending on the situation and with whom you interact. Dr. Paul Hersey and Dr. Ken Blanchard called it "Situational Leadership." The right leadership style will depend on the person or group being led.

> *There is no single 'best' style of leadership.*
>
> *- Dr. Paul Hersey and Dr. Ken Blanchard*

Employees might require different levels of direction and support based on their competence, commitment, maturity, and personality. For instance, you might employ a more autocratic style when dealing with employees who prefer direct instructions or junior employees with low skills. Alternatively, a more delegative and participative approach could be used to foster autonomy in teams and to empower more experienced employees.

Take a moment to reflect on your leadership style and gain inspiration from the initiatives shared in this book to lead with more positivity. You can improve your leadership approach by promoting positive emotions, focusing on a healthy feedback culture, managing stress, and cultivating emotional intelligence. These efforts will enable you to lead with greater positivity and authenticity. It's not about being the perfect leader (let's be clear, that doesn't exist); it's about finding the way that works for you, aligns with your values, and allows you to be authentic enough in the workplace.

Once you've identified your leadership style, the next step is to ensure your team understands it too.

IDEA 67

COMMUNICATE YOUR LEADERSHIP STYLE

Once you have a better overview and awareness of your leadership style, it's important to communicate it with your team, especially if you are new to a position or have new team members.

I have seen many employees destabilized and frustrated as they didn't understand their new leaders' behaviors. Some are introverts, others extroverts.

Some need to understand the big picture, while others are more analytic and need to understand the numbers first.

I remember a client from a medium-sized company in the healthcare industry telling me: *"My new manager didn't communicate his expectations with a strong focus on numbers and details. I came well prepared for our first monthly meeting, but I gave him the big picture and not the details he expected – of course, the meeting didn't go as expected, and we didn't start off on the right foot…"*

How many of you have been in a similar situation? With clear communication from the beginning, many meetings and monthly reviews could have gone much better.

As a leader, the goal is not to say, *"I am like this, and I want this. Full stop!"*

The goal is to manage expectations, create transparency, and be open about how you normally work, behave, and expect things to be. You can easily explain your leadership style, what's important to you, and what your values as a leader are. It's a conversation and not a monologue. Try also to understand your team members, their working styles, and the different personalities you have in the team.

Here are some sentences to use to start the conversation:

- *As we are a new team, I think it's important to understand how everyone works. For example, I am usually very analytical/I usually like to see the big picture first/I need to understand the numbers first.*
- *I do value feedback a lot, so I have an open-door policy. Are you comfortable giving constructive and positive feedback? Is it part of the team's culture?*
- *I usually set clear goals and allow freedom on how to achieve them. How do you feel about that?*
- *Proactive communication from all sides is very important to me. How do you normally communicate in the team?*
- *I have to admit that I have a tendency to forget things, so do not hesitate to remind me if I don't get back to you in a reasonable time frame.*
- *If you have the impression that I am micromanaging too much, please feel safe to address it openly.*

It might not always be easy to have such conversations and share your leadership style with clear communication, authenticity, and transparency. Still, working and growing together as a team is always better.

Authentic Leadership Is Linked to Emotional Intelligence

Do you remember the four domains of Emotional Intelligence (EI) discussed in the previous chapter?

Self-Awareness – Self-Management
Social Awareness – Relationship Management

EI is a cornerstone of authentic leadership. It helps leaders become more self-aware and empathetic, enabling them to effectively understand and manage their own emotions and the emotions of others. Through this self-awareness and empathetic approach, leaders can establish transparency and trust between themselves and their teams, which are essential components of authentic leadership. Moreover, high EI allows leaders to remain true to their values and ethics, thus reinforcing their authenticity.

Reflecting on your own authenticity at work is vital.

IDEA 68

WHAT DOES IT MEAN FOR YOU TO BE AUTHENTIC?

Authenticity is a vital element of modern leadership, though it can be unclear in the workplace. According to the Cambridge Dictionary, authenticity means *"The quality of being real or true."* However, it's essential not to misinterpret it.

**Being authentic is not about
being too straightforward
and sharing all our deepest
emotions and thoughts.**

Being authentic at work means being true to ourselves while also maintaining boundaries and professionalism.

Why is authenticity so important? Employees want to connect with their leaders and be inspired by honest and approachable people. Being authentic helps others feel connected and relate to you, which leads to more happiness in the workplace. Finding the right and healthy balance is crucial.

Take a moment to reflect on these questions:

- *What does it mean for you to be authentic at work?*
- *Are you an authentic leader/colleague?*
- *How can you be more authentic with your colleagues if you need to?*

IDEA 69
WHAT DO YOU WANT PEOPLE TO REMEMBER YOU FOR?

This question often generates buzz in my sessions. I see many leaders having *a-ha!* moments during this self-reflection exercise.

We have to rethink our leadership image. Sometimes, we are so caught up in our hamster wheel that we do not take the time to reflect on and analyze what we project.

**Keep in mind and consider the gap
between the image that others have of you
and the image you would like to project.**

Think about a great leader you've had in your career.

- *What made this person stand out?*
- *Why do you remember this particular leader?*
- *How did this leader make you feel?*

Hopefully, your employees and colleagues will also remember you for your leadership qualities: for the support you provide, your empathy, your skills as a coach, and your inspiring vision, rather than just remembering your bad moods or negative behaviors!

IDEA 70

LEARN TO LEAD WITH YOUR HEART AND NOT JUST YOUR MIND

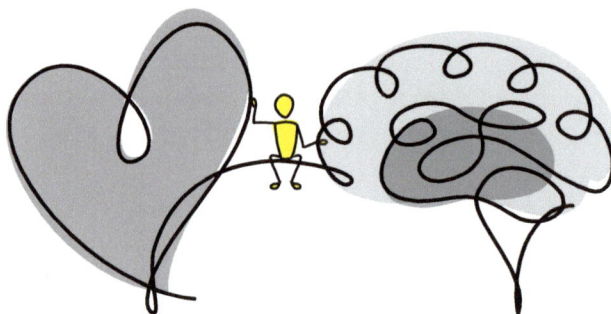

Leading with your heart, not just your mind, means including empathy, compassion, and emotional connection when making decisions or guiding a team. It does not imply that you are soft; you can be direct and goal-oriented yet still show empathy.

Leading with your heart emphasizes understanding and caring about the well-being and feelings of others rather than focusing solely on logic, metrics, and efficiency. It involves using emotional intelligence to create a supportive, trusting environment where people feel valued and motivated.

Self-awareness is the first step in this process. It involves recognizing and understanding your emotions and instincts. When you find yourself relying too heavily on logic and intellect, remind yourself to trust your feelings and intuition. This balance allows for more compassionate, inclusive, and authentic leadership.

LEAD WITH YOUR HEART...   ...NOT JUST YOUR MIND

IDEA 71

SWITCHING
FROM BOSS TO COACH

Leaders need to be inspirational. Let's move away from being a boss to being a coach, a mentor, a supporter. *It's the Manager – Moving from Boss to Coach* by Gallup is an amazing book on this topic. Check the QR code for references.

According to the Gallup book, there are three requirements to transform managers into coaches:

1. **Establish expectations:** involve employees in setting goals related to their role, purpose, priorities, career growth, and well-being.
2. **Continually coach:** have ongoing conversations, provide feedback, be aware of your team members' strengths, and learn to manage conflict.
3. **Create accountability:** include regular progress reviews and integrate individual employee development with performance measurement.

In addition, I believe that a coaching mindset involves:

→ Caring and showing empathy
→ Fostering collaborative relationships
→ Continuous learning
→ Embracing new opportunities
→ Sharing knowledge
→ Asking for help
→ Getting over failure
→ Focusing on people and not only on tasks
→ Enabling others' potential

Are you a boss or a coach? In which area could you work to switch your leadership style towards being more of a coach?

IDEA 72

Apologizing at work can feel awkward and is often labeled as a sign of weakness. But it's the opposite! A sincere apology shows you've taken ownership of the situation or your role in it.

There are five parts to an effective apology:

1. Express remorse or humility.
2. Acknowledge what happened or your responsibility.
3. Offer empathy or an explanation.
4. Follow through with a solution, support, alternative, or compensation if possible.
5. Reassure that it is unlikely to happen again and/or close with grace.

An effective apology avoids blame and excuses. Let's move away from "I am sorry but …" or "It happened because …"

5 Examples to start a sincere apology at work

- *I understand that my mistake has created extra work for you, and I sincerely apologize.*
- *I take full responsibility for the confusion caused by my actions.*
- *I apologize for the delay. It is now my top priority to ensure it's completed today.*
- *I am truly sorry for what I said earlier; I understand that it may have hurt you.*
- *I apologize for the confusion caused by the incorrect information in the report.*

Then, explain what happened, commit to an improvement or a solution, and remember to thank the receiver for understanding or accepting the apology.

It's not only about what you say but also how you say it!

Pay attention to your body language to ensure that your words and body language are aligned and authentic. Saying *"I'm sorry"* with a smug smile or an attitude that doesn't match your words will come across as fake and manipulative.

Choosing the right time and environment will also make a huge difference. Waiting too long might be too late, and apologizing too soon might not give the other person enough time to digest the situation. Whether to apologize privately or publicly depends on the situation. As does the form of the apology. For a smaller mistake, an email or private message might be enough. However, if your mistake caused more damage, a face-to-face conversation in private or public might be necessary.

Of course, we shouldn't apologize for anything and everything. We know when we have made a mistake and should do something about it. Apologizing is part of our authenticity at work.

Developing Resilience at Work to Be a Better Leader

The word "resilience," which originally meant "the act of rebounding," was often used in reference to physical properties. Over time, the term evolved to include mental and emotional strength when facing adversity, particularly in psychological and sociological contexts. Today, resilience emphasizes adaptability and the ability to recover in challenging circumstances.

In leadership, your resilience is tested quite often.

Resilience is the ability to recover quickly from difficulties or adapt well to challenges and setbacks. Let's be honest, we face numerous challenges at work, such as deadlines, workload, stress, and constant changes, which constantly test our resilience.

One way to avoid burnout or falling into a negative cycle is to work on our resilience.

**We can't ignore our emotions.
We need to feel what we feel
and face what we face.**

It's about accepting the situation. Acknowledging and regulating our emotions, being able to take a step back, and having an open and positive approach to adapting will help us be more resilient.

However, we don't always react to challenges in the same way. The topic of resilience is vast, and many experts will have different approaches and coping techniques.

There is a great metaphor that sticks with me and has helped a lot of the teams I work with to develop their resilience:

> *You can either react as a tennis ball or a tomato.*
>
> *- Dr Chris Johnstone*

Let's explore it in the next idea.

IDEA 73

REACT AS A TENNIS BALL OR A TOMATO

I first heard about this metaphor from Dr Chris Johnstone, an expert on resilience and well-being.

When you squeeze a tennis ball, it gets smaller and becomes a little squashed, but then it returns to its original shape. This demonstrates resilience, as it is the ability to **Bounce Back** to normal after facing challenging times (such as reaching a deadline or finishing a project, in the context of the workplace). This is also known as Recovery Resilience. It's about returning to your old self after a challenging time.

On the other hand, when you squeeze a tomato, it does not return to its original shape. Instead, the seeds may be pushed out and potentially grow into a new tomato plant. This kind of resilience is about **Bouncing Forward**. It involves creating something new and different, learning from the challenge, and growing.

This is known as Transformative Resilience. This is the kind of resilience we need in an organization, especially during organizational change.

It's okay to act like a tennis ball or a tomato, depending on the challenges or changes you are experiencing. It helps a lot to visualize these two main types of resilience when facing a challenge. Ask yourself: Is this a situation where I should react like a tennis ball (to go back to normal in a while) or more like a tomato (to learn from a challenge and grow)?

Dr Chris Johnstone also refers to **Bouncing With**, called Adaptive Resilience. It is the ability to adapt to a situation, like bouncing with the waves and adapting to turbulences.

The last type is **Bouncing Outwards** or Spreading Resilience, where you share, expand, and transmit it.

**Having these four types of resilience in mind
when you are going through a situation,
a change, or a challenging time
might help you be more resilient.**

You need to find your own coping techniques to develop your resilience. According to many experts, developing good relationships at work, working on your emotional and physical well-being, having a sense of purpose and a clear vision, and maintaining a positive mindset will help you be more resilient. The ideas and initiatives shared in this book might also inspire you to create your own resilience toolbox.

In summary, resilience supports authentic leadership by enabling leaders to navigate challenges with integrity, build trust, inspire others, and maintain emotional balance. These qualities create a strong foundation for effective and authentic leadership.

To conclude this chapter on leadership, I have asked Natalie Robyn, former automotive executive and CEO of the FIA (Federation Internationale de l'Automobile), to share her view on what it means to lead with authenticity and positivity.

Embracing Authenticity as a Female Leader

Interview with Natalie Robyn, Former Automotive Executive and FIA CEO

I had the amazing opportunity to interview Natalie Robyn, a former automotive executive and FIA (Federation Internationale de l'Automobile) CEO, about her leadership style. Natalie is a working mother who has mainly worked in male-dominated industries. She held C-level positions at companies like Volvo, Nissan, and DaimlerChrysler and was recently the first CEO of the Federation Internationale de l'Automobile (FIA).

It was essential to me to have such an inspirational leader and role model in this chapter. Natalie shares her vulnerability, struggles, and valuable tips for being an authentic leader and leading with more positivity.

> **Aurelie Litynski:** *Natalie, what does it mean for you to be an authentic leader?*
>
> **Natalie Robyn:** *Funny enough, I started my career 20 years ago by not being entirely authentic at work. As I was in a male-dominated industry, and most of the time the only female, I found myself mimicking some behaviors I thought were right. I noticed that I dressed like my male colleagues, spoke like them in meetings, and had typical male behaviors (which we would consider typical at that time – nowadays, it's completely different).*
>
> *And at one point, I realized it was not me! What's the point of faking in order to belong?*
>
> *As a female leader, I have been in situations that are completely inappropriate nowadays.*
>
> *So I asked myself: Is it what I want to do and what I want to go through?*
>
> *Who do I want to be? What kind of leader do I want to be?*

Thanks to mentors and role models throughout my career and the experience I gained over the years, I have been able to embrace my authenticity. I stopped trying to impress or fit in. It was just much easier to be me. For me, being authentic means that I am the same person at home and at work, being able to express myself, and giving visibility to others around me. It's you being you!

On top of that, it made me realize the responsibility I have as a leader to foster a positive work culture where especially young women and men can embrace their authenticity from the beginning of their careers.

Aurelie: *In your view, what key elements do you believe are essential for cultivating a positive work culture within teams?*

Natalie: *Especially when taking on a new leadership role in a company, my first priority is to bring the best people together. Before introducing any new initiatives or changes in the way we work, I focus on getting to know my team better and building a positive team atmosphere. During team meetings and social gatherings, I make a conscious effort to be authentic and true to myself, using my "American" sense of humor to help create a relaxed environment and connect with others on a deeper level. Of course, this became easier for me as my career progressed.*

I emphasize the importance of honesty with my teams, acknowledging that they might have more expertise than me in certain areas. From the start, I encourage people to speak up. Particularly if they consider something I say wrong. After all, being a leader is not about having all the answers. I often say, "There is nothing I love better than you proving me wrong with good facts and figures."

Having lots of human touchpoints with my teams helps me to create a healthy environment at work. Starting with a genuine "How are you doing at the moment?" speaking about their private life if open to it, and not only about work. Having regular face-to-face interactions such as 1:1 meetings and team-building activities helps me to create a human-centric culture with my team.

Aurelie: *What's the one thing you are specifically working on regarding your leadership style?*

Natalie: *I am especially trying to listen more actively. I speak quite a lot, and without realizing it, I can take up a lot of space. So, my goal is to talk less and listen more.*

Something else that's important and that I could work on is networking more. I am super social in my own network, but I stay in my comfort zone. I should get out there and attend more events to meet new people. It's hard work, but I realize that it's important to be a good leader. It will also help me to better understand the world, the market, and the bigger picture, and meet new people.

Aurelie: *What's your final advice for other leaders striving to implement a positive leadership style?*

Natalie:

➡️ *Be kind: Kindness is often the foundation for building good relationships. Let's be kind to people regardless of their responsibility and seniority in the company.*

➡️ *Have fun: We spend more time at work than at home, and it's crucial to feel good and have fun in the workplace. Bring humor into the mix; a shared laugh or a light-hearted smile makes people feel comfortable and forges connections.*

➡️ *Get to know the people around you: Speak with the people who work for you, get to know them, and know who the people in the different layers below are. It might help you discover future talents.*

I am a true believer that you should build the environment you want to work in!

Aurelie: *Being an authentic leader might mean accepting that sometimes we must end work relationships. I spoke to Natalie a few days after the media announcement that she would leave her position as CEO at FIA, and we had an interesting conversation about the offboarding:*

Natalie: *When starting your career, it can be challenging to leave a company if you feel like you don't belong, aren't being heard, or don't fit in with the organization's culture. As you gain more experience, you start to understand the environments where you can excel and make an impact, in alignment with your likes and dislikes. I learned early on that you usually can't change your manager, so you either adapt or move on.*

Clear communication is always very important. If you are unhappy with your work environment, it takes courage and willingness to speak up and find a solution. Cultivating a culture of open communication is crucial in finding a solution and it is important for yourself and your organization. Talk to your manager and try to explain why the situation is not ideal for you in the most objective way possible. Try to adapt and improve the situation, but know your limits and when it's time to move on for your own well-being, your career, and the organization itself. This could mean finding a new role within the company or outside of it. It's recognizing the career path you want to take and evaluating whether the company you are in will facilitate that path. It is important to find the power to say, "We have different visions and ways of working, so let's move on in the best way."

I recognize this is dependent on each individual's situation, of course. That's why it's important first to try to find a solution, understand what's really important for you, and know your market value. It's not easy, but at some point, you likely need to get ready to make a jump!

Every work experience is a huge learning opportunity. It will help you better evaluate your next step and ask the right questions during your future interviews to determine whether the culture and leadership style fit your values and authenticity.

— Natalie Robyn, Former Automotive Executive and FIA CEO

Natalie's example showcases perfectly one of the most important traits of high-level leaders mentioned in this chapter: authenticity in the sense of staying authentic with one's values and beliefs, even if that implies tough decisions.

We have seen in this chapter that authentic and positive leadership is not something given or pre-defined. Leaders can and should work on understanding their leadership style, adapting to specific situations, communicating with authenticity, and strengthening resilience. These are all distinct and important skills that can elevate the game and deliver better team performance by combining business drive and positive personal impact.

In the next chapter, we'll dive into how a healthy feedback culture encourages transparency, mutual respect, and personal development, setting a standard for the entire team.

CHAPTER HIGHLIGHTS

✔

Positivity is not just a personality trait but a skill that can be cultivated, and it significantly impacts leadership success.

✔

Leaders greatly influence their teams' mental health and workplace culture, highlighting the importance of positive and mindful leadership.

✔

Recognizing your leadership style (e.g., transformational, coaching, servant) is critical for self-awareness and adaptability.
Clear communication about your leadership style fosters better relationships and expectations within the team.

✔

Authentic leadership, supported by emotional intelligence, builds trust and connection, making leaders more relatable and effective.

✔

Resilience, both recovery and transformative, is vital in handling challenges and growing as a leader.

LET'S TAKE ACTION

➡ Reflect on your leadership style: What leadership style do you currently practice? How does it influence your team's performance and morale? Is there room for improvement?

➡ How can you improve your emotional intelligence to become a more authentic and positive leader?

➡ Think of a recent challenge you faced at work. Did you react as a "tennis ball" (bouncing back) or a "tomato" (bouncing forward and growing)? How can you build more resilience?

Access additional resources by scanning the QR code.

YOUR THOUGHTS
YOUR JOURNEY

Capture your insights, ideas, and action steps as you make this journey your own.

8

SHAPING
A HEALTHY
FEEDBACK
CULTURE

Feedback:
A Love-Hate Relationship

Feedback shouldn't be perceived as something negative or super formal; instead, it should be an integral part of the team's culture.

But let's face it: We all feel differently about feedback. Feedback can evoke a range of emotions and reactions, depending on our personal experiences and stories. We've all experienced this one way or another.

Receiving feedback might take you straight back to your time at school:

You're standing in front of the class, your stomach twisting in knots as you nervously present your project. Then, bam! Your teacher delivers feedback like a hammer, no empathy, no mercy. Suddenly, you feel like you could disappear, wishing the floor would swallow you whole. (Ah, the joys of teenage angst, right?)

Yet, this classic scenario could go in a different direction:

You're presenting your project, and your teacher offers feedback like a friendly guide, explaining where you need to improve and cheering you on with helpful advice. You walk away feeling empowered, ready to conquer the world – or at least the next assignment.

It might also take you back to your professional experiences:

You're presenting your ideas to the team. Suddenly, your new boss critiques your work with all the directness of a blunt tool, leaving you feeling deflated and small. But then, there's that one colleague who offers feedback like a guiding light, nudging you towards improvement with kindness and support.

Moments like these remind us how feedback can shape our professional journeys. They may trigger feelings of self-doubt, frustration, and, worse, imposter syndrome.

However, when given and received effectively, feedback can inspire positive change and growth.

So, what's your story with feedback? Is it more of a love or hate relationship?

Take a moment to reflect on your past experiences and how they have shaped your perception of the feedback process.

Why Is Giving Feedback So Important?

Feedback can inspire us to make positive changes or continue on a path that's already working well for us. Whether it's constructive criticism or a glowing review, feedback can be a real game-changer in the way we approach our goals and behaviors. Giving feedback requires bravery, dedication, and time. By teaching employees and leaders to cultivate a culture of feedback, organizations can create an environment that emphasizes continual growth and improved performance. It is one of the best ways to help employees thrive.

In a nutshell, feedback inspires individuals to change or maintain their behaviors.

Well-meaning feedback typically falls into two categories:

- **Constructive Feedback:** to highlight areas for improvement and encourage learning and growth.
- **Positive Feedback:** to recognize strengths and successes and provide encouragement.

Establishing a healthy feedback culture can significantly enhance relationships among colleagues and foster trust. Research shows that giving positive feedback not only increases happiness at work but also reduces stress and enhances productivity.

In a study conducted by the Harvard Business School[1], participants were asked to solve problems. Prior to this task, about half of the participants had received an email from a coworker or friend that described a time when the participant was at their best. The study found that those who read positive statements about their past actions were more creative in their approach, more successful at problem-solving, and experienced less stress compared to their counterparts. In other words, "when you think you can, YOU CAN."

FACT CORNER

According to an employee engagement report from WorkLeap-Office Vibe[2] using answers from a sample of approximately 50,000 people in 150 countries:

➡️ **83% of employees** think it's better to give someone praise than a gift.

➡️ **32% of employees** have to wait more than three months to get feedback from their manager. While most managers hate giving feedback, employees are actively looking for it.

➡️ **62% of employees** wish they received more feedback from their colleagues. It's not only managers who should be giving feedback – it's important to create a culture of feedback in your organization where everyone is helping everyone get better.

➡️ **64% of employees** think the quality of the feedback they receive should be improved. More important than the act of giving feedback is making sure that it's high quality.

These numbers prove that a healthy feedback culture involves regularly giving and receiving feedback in various forms. It shouldn't just come from the leadership team; feedback should be a reciprocal process. It's also crucial to understand how to provide high-quality feedback.

Feedback is not about making people feel good

Well-done feedback or praise is sincere (do it if you mean it), meaningful (praise people for something worth praising), and specific (tell them what was good).

Fake recognition is the worst!

It's important to avoid "fake recognition" or "toxic positivity" – feedback should be meaningful and constructive. Sometimes, we do have the urge to make people feel good, and sometimes, we avoid confrontation. Saying "*great job*" might be easier than giving structured, detailed, and thoughtful feedback to make them grow.

Receiving real positive feedback is crucial to our learning curve. We often know what's wrong or what we need to improve, but it's essential to realize and focus on what's working to support our development. On the other hand, harsh feedback will not help people thrive and excel. Strong negative comments can create defensive reactions. It is important to provide constructive criticism in a respectful and considerate manner.

In this chapter, we'll explore different feedback methodologies using positive psychology to adapt your feedback culture. Giving and receiving feedback in a way that makes a difference goes hand in hand with a culture of trust.

Let's Analyze Your Feedback Style

Understanding your feedback style is the first step toward making it more effective—take a moment to reflect on how you typically give feedback:

- *Are you direct?*
- *Do you demonstrate empathy?*
- *Are you comfortable revealing your vulnerabilities?*
- *Do you prefer to keep emotions off the table?*
- *Are you freestyle and using your instinct?*
- *Or maybe you are structured and apply a specific model?*

Below are feedback models that are commonly known and used across organizations:

- **STAR** model: **S**ituation, **T**ask, **A**ction, **R**esult
- **DESC** model: **D**escribe, **E**xpress, **S**pecify, **C**onsequences
- **AIR** Model: **A**ction, **I**mpact, **R**equest
- **BOOST** model: **B**alanced, **O**bjective, **O**bserved, **S**pecific, **T**imely
- **START – STOP – CONTINUE**: Something I would like you to **start/stop/continue** doing is …

➡ **Feedback Sandwich**: Start with positive feedback, then constructive, and finish with positive. This method can be tricky depending on how it's done. Most of the time, the feedback giver might feel good about it. However, it can be confusing for the recipient and may compromise the credibility when delivering positive feedback.

Take a minute to reflect on your team and company; which of these models do you see most used?

Analyze **your** style and the methodology you use.

Consider how you might be perceived when giving or receiving feedback.

On top, ask yourself:

- ○ *Have you received praise and recognition lately?*
- ○ *When was the last time you praised your colleagues/direct report?*

It can be challenging to ask for feedback if we don't provide feedback ourselves. Remember that feedback is a two-way street, so let's strive for a balance between giving and receiving.

While these models are well organized and mainly coherent, we could leverage the principles of positive psychology to create a more substantial impact when giving feedback. Let me explain some techniques in detail.

Apply Positive Psychology When Giving Feedback

Using positive psychology when giving feedback is an effective approach that involves emphasizing individual strengths, acknowledging emotions, encouraging personal growth, ensuring psychological safety, and fostering a constructive and supportive environment.

Regardless of the methodology you use, remember to incorporate positive psychology to provide effective and impactful feedback that promotes growth and development.

I've selected five different ways to make feedback more impactful:

IDEA 74

TURN THE "YOU" INTO THE "I"

Often, when we engage in a conversation, and especially with constructive feedback, we tend to use the word "YOU" to address the person in front of us. This can make the other person feel attacked, and they may become defensive.

To avoid this, it's better to focus on our emotions and express how we feel about the other person's behavior.

Instead of starting your feedback with "YOU"	Rephrase it by turning the "YOU" into "I"
YOU didn't send me the report on time	I felt quite stressed when I received the report at the last minute
YOU were not clear in your email	I am concerned by the email you sent to the client this morning
YOU have to ...	I am confused, I thought we agreed on ...

This way, we are expressing our feelings, and it's harder for the other person to argue with them. I often use the Feelings Wheel website to find the right words for my emotions. We mostly use the same vocabulary to express our emotions, and I find this wheel very practical to express myself, especially in difficult conversations.

Scan the QR code to gain access to the Feelings Wheel and choose the right emotions to support your feedback.

IDEA 75

This technique was first introduced by Bob Champman, CEO of Barry-Wehmiller, and then popularized by Simon Sinek and Kristen Hadeed, both renowned bestseller authors.

FBI = Feelings – Behaviors – Impact

The FBI is a tool that can be used for both critical conversations and recognition.

COMPONENTS OF SUCCESSFUL FEEDBACK

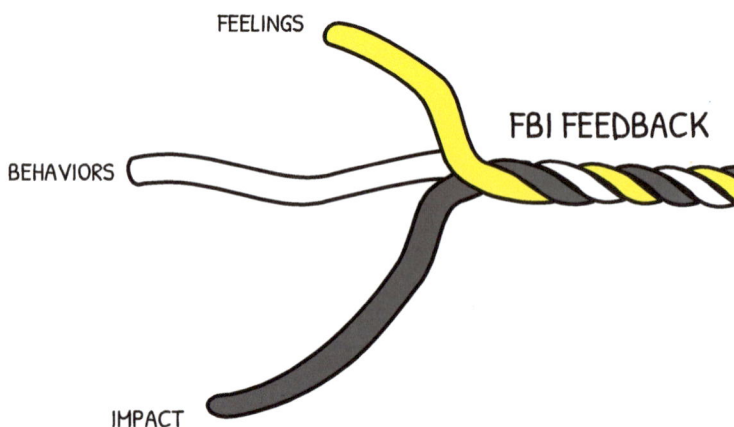

FEELINGS

FBI FEEDBACK

BEHAVIORS

IMPACT

➡ Express your **feelings.**

Express how you feel about the specific situation or behavior.

Be specific when sharing your feelings (use the Feelings Wheel previously explained for help). For example:

- ○ *I was quite stressed during the meeting when …*
- ○ *I am anxious regarding …*
- ○ *I am concerned about …*

- ○ *I was inspired by ...*
- ○ *I am so proud of ...*

⟹ Share the **behaviors** that caused that feeling.

It's important to let the other person know the specific actions they did that caused you to feel a certain way. The more detailed and specific you can be in communicating this, the better.

⟹ Speak about the **impact** that behavior might have in the future.

You might show them the consequences of their action (negatively or even positively).

How to apply the FBI method:

Let's put it into practice. Here are two examples of FBI for both positive and constructive feedback. I highlighted the FBI parts in bold.

Instead of saying:	Apply the FBI:
Great meeting this morning.	*I was truly impressed with your presentation this morning. Your idea was well explained and presented in such a clear and confident way that it inspired the entire team. I had the feeling that everyone left the room motivated and excited about the project. Great job!*
You changed your mind again.	*I am completely confused because in our last meeting, you requested (X), and when the team did it, you rejected it without explanation. It has happened quite often lately, and I am afraid that the team will lose their motivation and stop caring at some point.*

After such a FBI Feedback, pause and allow the person to respond. If they go into confrontation mode, repeat the FBI by starting again with your feelings.

Check out, by scanning the QR code, Simon Sinek's explanation of the FBI technique in his talk about effective confrontation.

By articulating your emotions and describing specific behaviors and their impact, you make it more difficult for the person to argue. Initiating the conversation in this manner can lead to a more productive exchange than immediately assigning blame.

Go further than the FBI:

Once you've developed your FBI, go deeper into the conversation, as real feedback is a genuine conversation and not a monologue. Use sentences such as:

- *I would love to know your perspective; what do you think of that?*
- *Does my example make sense to you?*
- *What's your plan to improve it?*
- *How can I support you?*
- *What are your key takeaways from this conversation?*

Depending on the situation, focusing on past mistakes may not contribute anything to the present circumstances. Instead, using the Feedforward technique would be more beneficial.

IDEA 76

FEEDFORWARD INSTEAD OF FEEDBACK

Another impactful method I often use is the Feedforward technique.

While typical feed**back** focuses on past events, feed**forward** concentrates on possibilities for the future. It focuses on future improvements rather than dwelling on past mistakes, and it provides suggestions aiming to help the receiver develop their skills.

Feedforward is particularly useful in ongoing professional development and coaching scenarios, providing a constructive and motivating way to look at growth and improvement.

In some scenarios, it can be more impactful to look to the future rather than the past.

How to apply the Feedforward method:

Instead of saying:	Apply the Feedforward:
You talked way too fast during your presentation!	*Next time you present, try pausing after each slide; it will help you re-balance, and your delivery will be more effective.*
I have the feeling you are always busy and struggling with your workflow.	*I realize how busy you are at the moment, so consider using project management tools to prioritize your tasks and manage your workload. I personally use the time boxing technique and see amazing results; it can also be efficient for you.*

Using Feedforward will help your team grow and achieve positive change; it helps focus on solutions – not problems.

As soon as you start applying these methods – Turn the YOU into the I, FBI, Feedforward – you will feel the incredible impact they can have on the people you work with.

But how about the feedback you receive? Collecting feedback is as important as giving it.

Let's explore a fun way to do it:

IDEA
77

When I need to collect instant feedback during a full-day workshop or longer session, I implement the Happiness Door, developed by Management 3.0.

The Happiness Door is a great technique to enhance team collaboration, employee engagement, and instant feedback.

How to use the Happiness Door:

➡ Choose a strategic place where all participants can see it. (It can be directly on the door, on the windows, or on a flipchart at the front of the room.)

➡ Draw on three Post-it notes with the same color: a happy smiley (at the top of the door), a neutral smiley (in the middle), and a sad smiley (towards the bottom of the door).

➡ Then give the participants other Post-it notes in different colors.

➡ Participants can give instant feedback about the session, something more specific, or how they feel during the day.

➡ They can either place it towards the top of the door for positive feedback or towards the bottom for more constructive feedback.

➡ It can be adapted for remote teams: Use the same principles on an online whiteboard or any collaborative platform.

Seeing the tendency for positive and constructive feedback on the door is very hands-on. It allows the facilitator or workshop leader to evaluate instant feedback, address it directly, and adapt if needed.

When I have a full-day workshop, I usually introduce it before the morning break and ask participants to add their feedback throughout the day. It allows me to gauge the room and react to their constructive feedback.

Check out some visuals by scanning the QR code and selecting this chapter.

Giving and receiving feedback shouldn't happen only once or a few times a year. It should be part of your company's culture or, at the very least, part of your team's culture.

IDEA
78

I'm frequently asked, in my sessions on feedback:

"How should I balance positive feedback with negative feedback?"

In my opinion, there is no ideal ratio of positive to negative feedback. It depends on the situation and the individual, but it should always be sincere and valuable. That said, I believe the worst approach would be giving two fake positive feedback just to deliver a constructive one.

One approach that has helped many leaders and employees I work with is visualizing the Feedback ATM. This is a way of thinking about feedback as if it were an emotional bank account.

Like a regular bank account, we want to keep our emotional bank account in the positive. This means:

➡ We need to make deposits (such as recognition, praise, kindness, and positive feedback),

➡ and also make withdrawals (such as constructive feedback, challenging conversations, and feedforward).

How's your emotional bank account looking?

Do you need to go to your Feedback ATM to make the balance positive?

The Basis to Make Feedback Part of Your Team's Culture

Regardless of the methodology you choose for your feedback, keep in mind:

➡️ Creating an environment of psychological safety and trust is the foundation.

➡️ It should be a healthy exchange and not a confrontation or a conflict – it's a dialogue.

➡️ Feedback is a two-way street: give and receive.

➡️ Establish a common objective to set clear expectations and have meaningful conversations.

➡️ Train people to give feedback: Teach them to use positive psychology and to give feedback effectively.

➡️ Train people to receive feedback (we are all triggered when we receive constructive feedback; we need to learn how to recognize and deal with our triggers).

➡️ Be specific rather than general and ambiguous.

➡️ Be sincere and authentic, instead of faking your feedback.

➡️ Make it a norm and not an exception once or twice a year.

➡️ Check in with the receiver to make sure you have a common understanding.

Giving and receiving feedback should be part of your team's culture. It should be done regularly and not always in a super official manner.

Here are different ways and formats you can use to enhance feedback in teams:

➡️ Start your monthly team meeting with a feedback round.

➡️ Include a FBI or Feedforward in your next 1:1 sessions.

➡️ Ask people to give you feedback on a previous task during an informal discussion or in a 1:1.

➡️ Create a Happiness Door or a Feedback Wall in the office so everyone can share feedback.

- Design a positive feedback wall in your online collaborative platform where employees can highlight the work of a colleague.
- Create a specific feedback channel in your preferred communication platform.
- Announce customer feedback in your newsletter, on a wall in the office, or during meetings.
- Use the spinning wheel (explained in Chapter 5) to choose a team member who will receive a "positive shower": lots of positive remarks from others.
- End your meeting with a closing round. Ask three questions at the end of the meeting:
  - *What went well?*
  - *What could have gone differently?*
  - *Any other ideas to improve?*

Choose the right format; the most important thing is to make it an integral part of your team's culture.

If you need to confront a team member and have a difficult conversation, make sure to:

- Prepare your FBI feedback well: You might even want to write it down to make sure you remember all the points you want to cover.
- Regulate your emotions before the conversation (using the box breathing technique explained in Chapter 9 might help).
- Focus on specific actions and behaviors instead of highlighting their personality traits.
- Use clear language and be direct in your delivery without taking too long to get to the point.

How do you feel when you receive feedback? Do you feel attacked, defensive, or overwhelmed? It's not always easy to receive feedback, and we need to pay attention to certain points.

How to Receive Feedback?

As already explained previously, we all have a feedback story, and it can influence the way we accept feedback. Our reactions are often related to our past experiences.

Usually, when emotions like anger, frustration, or sadness come up during receiving feedback, there is more to the story.

If you are giving feedback and the receiver has **a strong emotional reaction**, invite them to tell you more about why they are feeling that way.

➡ Show empathy, understanding, and compassion.

➡ You might need to give the feedback receiver time, a quick break, or come back to it later.

If you are receiving feedback and **find yourself feeling emotional**, it can be helpful to play the authenticity card.

➡ You can explain why you're having such a strong reaction,

➡ or ask for a quick break to get in a better headspace for the conversation.

Of course, this isn't always possible. You might be in a situation where a colleague or manager gives **harsh or unfounded feedback** and makes you feel intimidated or defensive with their comments. Then, you can try to:

➡ Stay calm and acknowledge the feedback without immediately reacting to any provocations (to avoid fast escalation).

➡ Ask for clarification and specific examples to better understand their points or concerns.

➡ Request a follow-up meeting to discuss further when everyone has had time to process and reflect.

➡ Try to take the constructive elements of the feedback and not the blame or harsh words.

➡️ If it escalates, seek support from a mentor, HR, or trusted colleagues. Collect all proof to make your point.

If you're **asking for feedback**, make sure to be clear and specific about what you're hoping to achieve.

➡️ For example, if you send a PowerPoint presentation to colleagues for feedback before an important meeting, let them know what aspects you want feedback on. This could include design, content, wording, or strategy.

➡️ By setting clear expectations, you can ensure that you receive feedback that's helpful and relevant to your goals.

Additionally, it's important to **thank the person** giving you feedback, regardless of whether it's constructive or positive.

➡️ Expressing gratitude for their honesty and taking the time to share their point of view can help build trust and strengthen relationships.

Keep in mind that the way you receive feedback can determine whether the person will give it again. In the end, receiving feedback will either help you grow or reinforce positive behavior.

Now, let's not mix feedback and complaints!

Handling
Chronic Complainers

Giving feedback and complaining is different.

We have to make sure that our feedback isn't just a complaint.

Are you a complainer?

Let's be honest, it's easy to complain, and it can feel quite good. As I had mentioned earlier, I used to be quite a big complainer. But is it effective? Most of the time, not really ...

Don't just complain, make it constructive!

It can be very challenging when facing colleagues who, instead of providing feedback, end up on a rant. Learning to deal with chronic complainers at work can be a game-changer.

What do you think chronic complainers need or want?

Unfortunately, traditional strategies like trying to cheer them up or suggesting solutions for their problems don't always work.

In many cases, complainers are looking for empathy and understanding. Often, they feel powerless in front of a situation and feel trapped in it.

By acknowledging the fact that the issue is a big problem for that person (if not necessarily agreeing with the content), we can take the first step towards improving the situation. Sometimes, people need to be understood and listened to before they can be cheered up.

Telling someone how to fix a problem is often the wrong approach. Instead, you can ask questions that make them think and encourage them to explore and experiment.

I find these three questions powerful for such a conversation:

- *What are the possible next steps you could take to tackle this problem?*
- *What support or resources do you need to resolve this?*
- *What outcome are you hoping for by sharing this with me?*

Another strategy that helps when someone complains or vents is to ask them:

- *Do you want me to listen to you vent, or do you want me to help you fix it?*

Try to set expectations right; sometimes, people "just" need to vent to feel better, and you "just" need to listen. A complainer wants to be heard, so listen to understand their concerns.

Set boundaries and limits.

Depending on the situation, you can even try to say something like:

- *Ok, feel free to vent for a few minutes, and then we can focus the discussion on solutions.*
  It gives clear structure and expectations.

- *This isn't the best time for this discussion. Let's schedule a proper meeting to talk about it.*
  It allows both parties to be fully available for the discussion and prepare or cool down if needed.

Just like complaining can become a habit, so can being appreciative, optimistic, and grateful. We can train our ability to be positive. Remember the idea of No Complaining Day in Chapter 2? It might be time to suggest it to your team!

What If Feedback Doesn't Work?

It's a common saying that getting older makes us wiser– and something we often learn with more experience is that we cannot change people. I can now definitely relate to that.

What we can do is show them what we see, inspire them, and then let them decide what to do with that insight. Giving constructive feedback is not about changing the person. It's about helping them grow. Then, of course, we need to take action if there is no response or improvement, especially in the workplace setting.

If you are a leader giving feedback and there are no results or improvements, reflect on these questions:

- *Have you used the right techniques to give your feedback?*
- *Have you set clear expectations?*
- *Do they have the tools they need to improve?*

For certain situations, it is helpful to set an improvement plan together and then give them ownership of it.

- *What will you do to improve X?*
- *What will be the impact?*
- *What is your plan to turn it around?*
- *By when will you turn it around?*
- *What happens if you don't achieve it?*

Then, the plan is clear for both sides.

If employees give feedback to leaders or their peers and there is no change, try to suggest solutions; using the Feedforward technique can be powerful for this situation:

- *Let's try to …*
- *Here are ideas on what we could do to make it work …*
- *Why don't we …*

Let's admit that the topic of feedback is crucial but also complex. It depends on many external factors such as the situation, team culture, personality, relationship, right timing, or our own triggers. Sometimes, we think we're giving feedback to help or with good intentions, but it can quickly turn into a toxic form of feedback.

The Toxic Forms of Feedback

Some people mistake feedback for compliments, while others view it as a chance to offer unsolicited advice.

I frequently collaborate with Christopher Lübbers, my personal speaker and communication coach. During our conversation about how overwhelmed I can sometimes become with feedback and its significance, Christopher introduced an intriguing perspective that I would like to feature in this book as it started to change my perspective.

Here is what Christopher shared:

> *Most of the leaders I coach receive tons of advice disguised as "feedback." They sometimes even feel like the other person is trying to fix a problem they don't actually have.*
>
> *While effective and meaningful feedback is indeed a powerful gift, many of us fail to understand what real feedback is meant to achieve. The single goal of constructive feedback is to create perspective and higher self-awareness for the receiver. It is not about fixing a problem, establishing truth, or "winning."*
>
> *So, when someone approaches you after a presentation saying, "Hey! Great presentation!" it's not feedback at all. You might feel good because you got a compliment, but you don't know what exactly was great about your presentation. If I were to ask you what specifically you'll repeat next time, you'd have a hard time pinpointing it.*
>
> *That comment was nothing more than someone trying to fulfill some social duty. They spend minimal energy to help you build perspective, perform better next time, or fix a blind spot. Sharing comments did more for them (seem generous) than for you (gain a new perspective).*
>
> *Another toxic form of so-called feedback is comments suggesting you have a problem that needs fixing, rating you, or judging you. It might sound like:*
>
> *"Here's what you should do," "That didn't really work, did it?" or "You need to be more responsive to your emails."*
>
> *All these comments make you feel bad and self-conscious. You either feel under pressure to answer your emails faster or obsess about finding out what "didn't work" or what you missed. Yet, they are labeled "feedback" and thus generously distributed.*
>
> *Let's assume the factual basis behind these comments is valid, and the distributor actually wanted to see a change in your behavior. For this change to*

happen, it is critical that you understand what actions made the person come to you and share these comments. Only understanding what exactly you did, triggering that comment, and what it meant for the other person will empower you to decide if you want to modify your behavior.

Effective feedback is never about the giver's needs, but always about the receiver.

Think about what perspective the receiver needs to gain to actually change their behavior, grow, or understand. When sharing feedback, do not focus on WHAT the success or problem was but on WHY it was a success or problem, and you'll see how the receivers will light up and feel empowered.

Being given clear paths for personal growth puts us in charge of our own happiness and success.

Instead of saying "Good job" to a colleague, you could add, "Here are two things that really worked for me."

Instead of saying, "You need to be more responsive," rather use the FBI technique previously explained: "When I don't hear from you, I worry that we are not on the same page."

Helping them to understand how they made you feel is empowering. They will be in a spot to decide whether it was their intention or not and eventually shift their behavior.

Know the difference between feedback, compliments, and advice, and you will play a pivotal role in developing others and creating a happier and more collaborative culture at work.

– Christopher Lübbers, Speaker and Communication Coach

CHAPTER HIGHLIGHTS

✔

Feedback can develop a range of emotions and reactions,
depending on our personal experiences and stories.

✔

Feedback inspires individuals to change or maintain their behaviors.

✔

Fake recognition is the worst –
feedback is not about making people feel good.

✔

Focus on emotions when giving feedback:
express how you feel about the other person's behavior.

✔

Feedback is a two-way street! It should involve both giving and receiving.
Use feedback regularly and in different formats.

✔

Make sure that feedback does not become a complaint.

✔

Feedback, compliments, and advice are three different things.

LET'S TAKE ACTION

➡ Next time you give feedback to a co-worker, try the FBI or Feedforward technique and write down how you feel about it and its impact.

➡ Reflect on your Feedback ATM – need to make deposits?

➡ How do you normally react when you receive feedback? Is there anything you need to adapt?

Access additional resources by scanning the QR code.

YOUR THOUGHTS
YOUR JOURNEY

Capture your insights, ideas, and action steps as you make this journey your own.

9

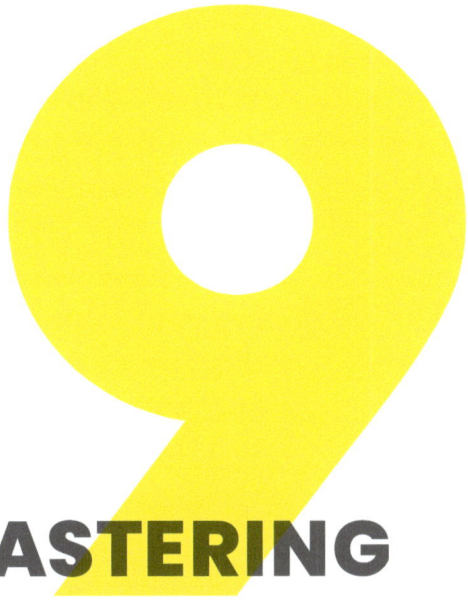

MASTERING STRESS & BOOSTING FOCUS

Stress: Enemy or Best Friend?

We all react to stress differently. A small amount of stress can be good for us, but too much stress can be detrimental. Whereas, no stress at all can lead to disengagement and boredom. Like most things in our life, we need to find a good balance.

Unsurprisingly, when we get too stressed at work, we are less efficient.

Stress can limit our capabilities. A stressed brain can lead to memory loss and reduced problem-solving effectiveness. Numerous studies[1] have shown the impact of chronic stress on our physical and mental health, which can increase absenteeism and reduce overall productivity. It's no secret anymore that workplace stress can affect both individual well-being and organizational performance.

**Stress can be viral.
Feeling stressed doesn't necessarily
require a concrete reason;
just one stressed colleague
can influence the entire team.**

This is due to our mirror neuron system, which causes us to mimic the emotions of those around us. Just as we imitate gestures (e.g., when someone yawns in front of you, you do the same automatically), we also imitate emotions. Being constantly surrounded by stressed individuals can lead to an increase in your own levels of cortisol, the hormone commonly associated with stress. When you see someone stressed, your brain can trigger the same response, even if you're not directly stressed yourself. Similarly, when witnessing a person express an emotion, such as happiness or sadness, mirror neurons can simulate that same emotion in your brain. These neurons don't only enable imitation; they also play a crucial role in fostering empathy, compassion, and social interactions. They help us recognize and understand the behavior of others.

People respond differently to stress: some are more sensitive to it, some don't cope well with stress, while others tend to offload their stress onto others. In the context of workplace, there are many factors to influence your stress. It's essential to reflect on your stress levels and understand the roots and consequences.

With the rise of burnout in the workplace, we have to recognize stress signs, use coping techniques, and create a safe environment in which to work at our best.

Recognizing and managing your emotions can greatly help you handle your stress levels. Everyone has different methods, but in general, taking care of ourselves by developing healthy habits and working more efficiently can help us manage workplace stress. I will explain both parts in this chapter: self-care and a smarter way of working.

Self-Care for Stress Reduction

Taking good care of yourself will significantly impact how you handle challenging emotions. There are many steps we can take for self-care to avoid or reduce stress. From getting a good night's sleep, maintaining a balanced diet, and exercising regularly to promoting positive emotions such as gratitude, there are many ideas you can add to your self-care toolbox!

By prioritizing self-care, employees and organizations can create a healthier work environment where productivity is sustained and burnout rates are significantly reduced.

In this section, I'll provide you with some self-care tips to help reduce your stress level. Remember that the goal is not to apply everything at once; the goal is to create your own stress management toolbox, which will enable you to better understand what you need to do – or pay attention to – in a stressful moment.

IDEA 79

10 QUESTIONS TO EVALUATE YOUR STRESS LEVEL

Identifying the sources of stress, how it manifests, and what your coping techniques are will help you better assess your stress level to manage it more effectively.

Here are ten self-reflection questions to evaluate your stress:

- *What aspects of your job do you find most stressful?*
- *How often do you feel overwhelmed, nervous, or stressed at work?*
- *Can you identify any specific tasks or responsibilities that consistently trigger stress?*
- *Have you noticed any physical symptoms that occur when you are stressed (e.g., headaches, back pain)?*
- *Does stress affect your sleep or eating habits?*
- *Do you find it difficult to concentrate or make decisions when stressed?*
- *What strategies do you currently use to manage stress at work?*
- *In the past month, how often have you felt unable to cope with everything you had to do?*
- *Do you feel comfortable discussing work-related stress with your manager, colleagues, or HR department?*
- *What changes could you make to help reduce your stress level?*

Take the time to reflect on these questions and start analyzing your stress level. Your answers will give a good indication and will help you take micro steps for improvement. If needed, you can also open up the discussion with those around you. These questions can also be used in 1:1 discussions, surveys, or annual reviews to assess an employee's stress levels.

Do you remember the initiative "Charge Your Battery" from Chapter 3 on well-being? It might be helpful to re-visualize your energy drainers and energy fillers.

IDEA 80

CALCULATE YOUR SLEEP DEBT

The connection between mental health and quality sleep is undeniable. Just as vital as eating and drinking, sleep is crucial for maintaining robust mental and physical health. Establishing a consistent sleep routine is essential. Studies[2] show that there is a strong correlation between sleep and emotional reactivity.

A lack of sleep leads to mood instability and emotional reactions.

- ○ *Do you know how much sleep you **need** during a workweek to be well-rested and at your best the next day?*
- ○ *And do you know how much sleep you actually **get**?*

The difference is your sleep debt!

Let's evaluate it in the next Expert Corner with sleep neuroscientist Dr. Els van der Helm.

EXPERT CORNER

With Dr Els van der Helm

Dr Els van der Helm, sleep neuroscientist, explains how to calculate our Friday morning sleep debt and gives us some techniques to improve our sleep:

Answer the following questions:

- ○ **Question A:** *How many hours of sleep do you get on a weeknight?*
- ○ **Question B:** *How many hours of sleep do you need to feel well-rested throughout the day?*

Now plug your answers for A and B into the following equation:

Friday morning sleep debt = $(5 \times A) - (5 \times B)$

What's your result?

Sleep-deprived individuals are less likely to engage in social activities, leading to loneliness and isolation, which impacts mental health and resilience.

What can you do if your sleep debt is too high? As Dr van der Helm recommends:

➡ Get a longer night; go to bed earlier, sleep in a bit longer
➡ Take a power nap (10–15 minutes) or even a recovery nap (90 minutes)

Sleep is your secret weapon
to adapt to the fast-paced world!
– Dr Els van der Helm

Source: Dr Els van der Helm[3].

In any case, it's important to establish a healthy sleep routine on a regular basis. I personally find the 10-3-2-1 rule quite practical to remember and apply:

The 10-3-2-1 rule:

- 10 hours before bed, no caffeine
- 3 hours before bed, no food
- 2 hours before bed, no work
- 1 hour before bed, no screens

Let's be honest: it might not always be easy to follow the 10-3-2-1 rule each night. However, being aware of it helps us apply it more consistently and allows us to establish a better sleep routine. Setting reminders to "wind down," stop using screens, and acknowledge that bedtime is approaching can be an effective way to adhere to this rule.

Making sure that we get a good night's sleep is crucial for our holistic well-being.

Let's explore another trick that is now part of my weekly routine to stay focused, handle my emotions, and help me to cool down when needed.

IDEA 81

ESSENTIAL OILS AT WORK

Nature supports us in many ways, and essential oils can be an invaluable resource in the workplace for individuals and teams. They offer a range of benefits, from enhancing focus and attention to reducing stress and promoting a positive atmosphere. I have been using essential oils at work for many years, and I asked my Aromatherapist, Marie Boutemy, to recommend four essential oils to help manage our emotions during a stressful day in the workplace.

"

Essential oils are concentrated extracts derived from plants, containing volatile organic compounds such as terpenes, alcohols, esters, ketones, and phenols. These compounds contribute to the unique scent and therapeutic properties of each oil. The biochemical molecules of essential oils interact with our body, mind, and emotions, offering various benefits. So, let's harness the power of these botanical wonders for some serious workplace magic!

Here are four different situations where you could use four different essential oils (with their botanical names) that may help improve workplace well-being:

➡ **Stress relief: Lavender** *(Lavandula angustifolia) to promote relaxation and reduce stress levels.*

➡ **Focus and attention: Laurel** *(Laurus nobilis) to help you bring your attention back on track.*

➡ **Memory: Rosemary** *(Rosmarinus officinalis) for a quick memory boost during tasks requiring mental clarity and retention.*

➡ **Quieting the mind: Petitgrain Bigarade** *(Citrus aurantium leaf) to help you cool off after a long meeting or a long day. For enhanced relaxation, consider combining it with lavender oil, especially in the evening.*

Two ways to use the above essential oils at work:

➡ *Diffuse up to five drops using an electric diffuser in your office for 15 minutes, up to three times a day – it will disperse the oil into the air for you to breathe it naturally. If you are in a shared office, make sure to check with your colleagues first if that's okay for them.*

➡ *Alternatively, take an "aromatic break" at your desk by slowly inhaling through the nose directly from the bottle for a minute while concentrating on your breathing.*

Safety Measures: *Essential oils are highly concentrated, and some may come with specific cautions or restrictions. Pregnant individuals, children, and those with specific health conditions should consult a healthcare specialist* *or a certified aromatherapist before using essential oils. Use essential oils according to recommended guidelines and avoid excessive exposure. Essential oils can be used in various ways, olfaction is the safest way.*

By incorporating essential oils into the workplace, employees can experience enhanced well-being and productivity while fostering a positive and harmonious environment.

Let's make work a little more fragrant and fun!

– Marie Boutemy, Aromatherapist

Combining the use of essential oils with breathing techniques is a perfect match:

IDEA
82

BOX
BREATHING

Box breathing, also known as square breathing or "the Navy SEAL breathing technique," is a breathing method used to manage stress, control emotions, and enhance performance.

Initially adopted by the United States military, this technique was designed to regain emotional control and improve concentration and focus before entering high-pressure situations. In box breathing, you inhale, hold your breath, exhale, and pause, each for four seconds.

Counting breaths helps keep the mind focused on the present, reducing distractions. Deep, rhythmic breathing increases the exchange of oxygen in the body and improves oxygen delivery to the brain, promoting clearer thinking and focus. The brief breath-holding phase allows oxygen to circulate more effectively and signals the body to relax. It also increases mindfulness and concentration, helping you gain better control over your breathing and emotions. Focusing on slow breathing reduces the production of stress hormones like cortisol, which can help achieve a calmer state of mind.

How to practice box breathing at work:

- Get into a comfortable position (stand or sit on a chair with a straight back and two feet on the ground)
- Inhale through your nose for four counts (1–2–3–4)
- Hold your breath in for four counts (1–2–3–4)
- Exhale slowly through your mouth for four counts (1–2–3–4)
- Hold again for four counts (1–2–3–4)
- Repeat this cycle multiple times (minimum one minute)

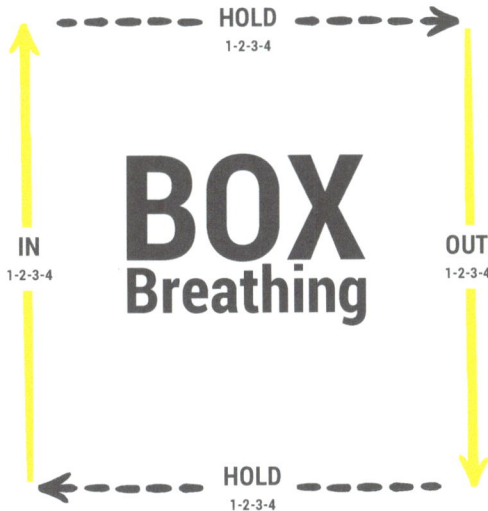

Check the box breathing video by scanning the QR code.

When to use box breathing:

- When feeling overwhelmed
- To manage chronic stress
- Regain focus if you are distracted
- To calm your nerves/anxiety before, for example, an important presentation
- When a colleague gets on your nerves, breathe before speaking
- Helping you fall asleep after a stressful day

I often do box breathing combined with the "power pose" before delivering a speech on a big stage in front of a large audience. A power pose is a confident, open body posture (like standing tall with hands on hips). Combining this pose with box breathing helps me to concentrate and control my stress levels.

You can practice box breathing before or even during an important meeting – it's hardly noticeable and can be done everywhere. I often recommend teams do it before a long workshop, especially if you need them to be engaged or during a brainstorming session if people are not focused and creative enough.

If you are more of an active person and cannot really stay seated at your desk, the next idea might be ideal.

IDEA 83

FROM SITTING TO CYCLING

Do you enjoy sitting in your office all day? This can be boring and unhealthy, especially for office workers who must stay in the same position behind their computers for long periods. Although we might move from our desk to a meeting room, lounge area, or stand up while working, we don't move much throughout the day, especially if we work from home.

The increased use of **under-desk walking pads** (a simple treadmill without handrails, small enough to fit in under a desk) or **under-desk bikes** (an adapted pedal set that fits under a desk) in offices makes a real difference in our physical and mental well-being. By exercising while working, you engage in a low-impact workout that doesn't just burn calories – it impacts your health, creativity, and mental focus and reduces stress.

At home or in the office, you can organize under-desk bikes or walking pad stations. Put an adapted bike or walking pad under a height-adjustable desk. It will help to:

➡ Improve your health as you engage in a low-impact workout to boost circulation and cardiovascular health.

- Boost your energy level as physical activities increase the blood flow and oxygen to the brain.
- Improve mental clarity and focus, and reduce stress as, while moving, you release hormones and neurotransmitters that help to clear mental fog, enhance mental concentration, and regulate emotions.

Various studies[4] have shown that walking can increase creative output by 60%. Participants performed better in creative thinking tasks while walking compared to sitting. Using a walking pad during the workday improved people's energy levels, reduced soreness, decreased hip and back pain, boosted mood, and enhanced focus and creativity.

Find your own balance and choose what kind of tasks you want to do while biking or walking. Biking might help while listening to a webinar, learning a new skill, or participating in a town hall meeting. Maybe you will find it useful to walk on a walking pad while brainstorming with your colleagues. Adapt it to your own way of working and use it when you need an energy boost.

Ludovic Pureur, Regional Vice President at Personify Health (formerly Virgin Pulse), shared his daily routine that uses an under-desk walking pad:

> *I always start my day with 30 minutes to an hour of walking at my desk. It energizes me right from the start and allows me to tackle my creative tasks before diving into my meetings. I never walk for more than an hour at a time, preferring to spread my walking sessions throughout the day to avoid soreness in my feet and legs. I usually have another session after lunch to boost my energy again, and I fit in smaller sessions depending on my meetings, tasks, and stress level. In total, I typically log between 8,000 and 14,000 steps a day without even noticing! It had a tremendous positive impact on my health – I can feel my back and core muscles are stronger, my posture has improved significantly, and it positively affects my moods, stress levels, and concentration. It's the best investment I've made in my professional life!*
>
> *- Ludovic Pureur, Regional Vice President at Personify Health*

Unable to set up a walking pad under your desk? Ensure you take a walk outside at least once a day, use the stairs instead of the elevator, prioritize walk-and-talk meetings, and promote group walking. Having an under-desk walking pad shouldn't keep you from doing these anyway!

Scan the QR code for examples of under-desk walking pads and bikes.

IDEA 84
BUILD YOUR STRESS MANAGEMENT TOOLBOX

I don't know about you, but on stressful and busy days, I tend to skip my breaks, grab a quick lunch, and multitask to finish everything at the same time. As a result, my mind gets foggy, and I can't think straight anymore. By the end of the day, I haven't achieved much and I feel frustrated. Can you relate?

This was me before creating my stress management toolbox! Studying positive psychology, stress management, and emotional intelligence made me realize the importance of being aware of your emotions and having the right tools in place to handle and regulate them before you become stressed.

Proactively planning and knowing what you need to handle challenging emotions will help you avoid getting stuck in a hamster wheel. Make a list of what YOU normally need to handle your stress better. It can be walking outside, doing burpees for five minutes, calling a friend to vent, meditating for five minutes, going for a run at lunchtime, or using fidgeting tools such as an anti-stress ball. Make this list accessible and visible so you can refer to it when you start to have a foggy brain and can't think straight anymore.

It's like having tools ready for when times get tough!

For instance, any morning when I have a busy day ahead or feel stressed when looking at my long to-do list, I schedule a short yoga break in my calendar to gently remind myself to do stretching movements. I am aware that taking five or ten minutes to move my body gently is part of my toolbox, and I usually feel calmer and more aligned, even if it is only five minutes. By having it on my calendar, I feel the positive pressure to actually do it. Another example is that I might begin a busy day with a long walk outside to expose myself to sunlight before starting a marathon of sessions and meetings. This helps me start the day on a positive note. In addition, exposure to daylight in the morning is known to boost mood, enhance concentration, and reduce cortisol levels (often known as the stress hormone).

Now it's your turn. Reflect on what should be in your toolbox. What helps you handle your emotions and decrease feelings of stress?

Download the illustration via the QR code to personalize your toolbox.

BUILD YOUR STRESS MANAGEMENT TOOLBOX

WHAT ARE YOUR OWN TOOLS?

Knowing which tools are beneficial for you will support you when you are under stress. Keep in mind that your toolbox evolves and needs to be adapted from time to time.

We could easily add ten more initiatives for self-care. We all have different ways to regulate our emotions. Some of us like to do intense sports, others like to meditate every day, and some people seem to cope with stress just fine. Being aware of your coping toolbox is the first step to handling your stress level at work.

Now that we've explored what you can do for self-care to reduce stress, let's look at the other aspect of managing stress – your work habits.

The truth is, we might not always be able to work less, but we can certainly strive to work smarter!

Work Smarter – Not Necessarily Less

In the workplace, there are many things beyond our control, and our workload might be one of them. For some of us, it's not always easy to manage our workload by refusing to add tasks to our long to-do list, so what we can do is focus on things we can control better: our way of working. Working smarter boosts our happiness at work by reducing stress and increasing efficiency, allowing for more meaningful engagement and accomplishment. Our feeling of progress will increase, as we'll explore in Chapter 10.

To increase productivity and work quality, there are several techniques that can be implemented. Firstly, it's helpful to consider what time of day you have the most energy.

IDEA 85

DISCOVER YOUR BIOLOGICAL PRIMETIME

Every individual has a unique body clock that influences what time their energy levels are most productive, referred to as their biological primetime. Some people prefer to wake up very early to tackle their most important tasks, while others find they work more efficiently in the evening. Since we are all different, our productivity does not occur at the same time of day.

Consider the following self-questions to help you discover your most productive time:

- *Are you a morning or evening person?*
- *When can you focus best at work?*
- *What time of the day are you the most creative?*
- *How's your energy level and motivation through the day?*
- *When are you at your best for thinking?*
- *Do you prefer to start your day with focused work, creative work, or shallow work?*

By tracking the time you spend on different tasks, your energy levels, feelings, and productivity, you can conduct a comprehensive analysis to divide your day into blocks:

- **Focused/deep work:** All about working intensively and without interruptions
- **Shallow work:** For routine or repetitive tasks you have to achieve
- **Open work:** For creative or strategic tasks
- **Communication/collaboration block:** To answer emails, participate in meetings, and collaborate with others

The goal is to be in sync with your peaks and your dips. You might need to align your focused work with the time of the day you are the most productive.

For example, I find it necessary to handle my emails and social media before beginning my focused work. It's difficult for me to concentrate deeply if I have pending important emails or social media posts to write. I know that I'm most productive for focused and creative work between 09:00 and 11:00 in the morning. Before and after lunch, I tend to do some shallow work (administration or repetitive tasks). My productivity increases again in the middle of the afternoon, especially after a quick walk outside.

Understanding this, you can schedule meetings and manage tasks around your most productive time to maintain high energy levels for focused work. At least you can give it a try!

Another important step in working smarter and enhancing focus is avoiding distractions.

IDEA 86

We can get quite distracted during a working day! Our most common distractions at work are often:

- → Co-workers
- → Smartphones
- → Emails, notifications
- → Social Media
- → Pointless Meetings
- → Multitasking

Looking at statistics, we can clearly see a tendency. Being distracted impacts our productivity. Different surveys and group discussions[5] showed that:

- → The average desk job employee loses 2.1 hours a day to distractions and interruptions.
- → It takes 23 minutes and 15 seconds to fully recover focus after a distraction.
- → Companies spend up to 31 hours a month in unproductive meetings.
- → Trying to focus on more than one thing at a time reduces your productivity by as much as 40%.

It takes time to recover from distractions:

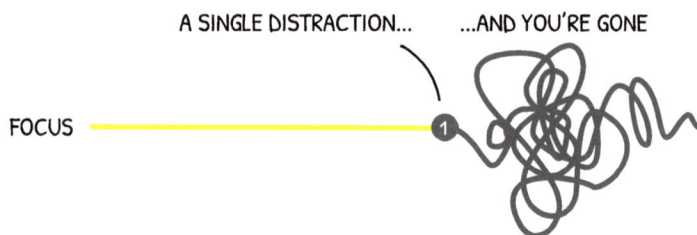

A SINGLE DISTRACTION...   ...AND YOU'RE GONE

FOCUS

As I learned in my trainings with the expert Nir Eyal on focusing at work, I realized that we mainly have two kinds of behaviors and triggers toward our actions. Understanding these concepts can help employees identify when they are being distracted and develop strategies to refocus on productive and meaningful activities. This awareness of traction versus distraction enables a more mindful approach to how we spend our time and energy.

Let's explore the keys to becoming "indistractable," as explained by Nir Eyal in the next Expert Corner.

EXPERT CORNER

With Nir Eyal

Nir Eyal, author of two bestselling books, thought leader on how psychology, technology, and business shape our habits and attention, shared powerful techniques to enhance focus in his fascinating book *Indistractable* and online course *The 4 Keys To Indistractable Focus*.

According to Nir Eyal, we have two kinds of behaviors toward our actions, reflecting our level of control and intentionality:

➡ **Traction:** Traction is any action that pulls you toward what you want to do, activities that you do with intent that move you closer to your goals.

➡ **Distraction:** Distraction is any action that pulls you away from what you intend to do, or actions that move you further away from your goals.

Then, we have two kinds of triggers toward the action:

➡ **External triggers:** Such as emails, notifications, meetings, phone calls, colleagues, etc.

➡ **Internal triggers:** The state of mind we try to escape, such as stress, anxiety, or boredom.

We seek for distractions to escape dissatisfaction.
– Nir Eyal

The four keys to "indistractable focus," according to Nir Eyal:

➡ **Master internal triggers:** Understand the root cause of distraction and learn to manage the discomfort that leads to it.
➡ **Make time for traction:** Plan your day with intention to guide your actions toward productive and meaningful activities, rather than being reactive to distractions.
➡ **Hack back external triggers:** Identify and reduce the external cues that lead to distraction, such as notifications from smart-phones or interruptions from colleagues.
➡ **Prevent distraction with pacts:** Create pre-commitments that block potential distractions and keep you on track.

Source: Nir Eyal's Book *Indistractable* and online course *The 4 Keys To Indistractable Focus*.[6]

Knowing this, start to reflect on your own behaviors:

○ *What are your most common external triggers?*
○ *What kind of internal trigger do you have and which state of mind are you trying to escape?*
○ *What are you normally doing to stay focused at work?*
○ *What else could you do to be less distracted and more focused?*

By scanning the QR code, you can access a template I've created to start track-ing your distractions. This will help you take action and minimize distractions.

I've selected some time management techniques, other initiatives, and meth-odologies to help you work smarter – adapt them to your own situation:

IDEA 87

Time boxing is, in my opinion, one of the best time management techniques, and it has completely changed my way of working.

The goal is to allocate a fixed time period, called a "time box," to a specific task or activity. It involves planning your day or week by assigning specific time slots to tasks before you start them. Essentially, you decide in advance what you are going to do and when you will do it. Planning is often a great way to distinguish between traction and distraction.

You can start small by allocating 30 minutes to an hour of focused work per day to your agenda. During this time, allocate a specific task: *working on project X, finishing my presentation for the management meeting, starting the budget for X, replying to all urgent emails* … Make sure you switch off notifications and handle external triggers during your time box.

Once you master the "beginner level" of time boxing, you can reorganize your whole to-do list using this technique.

- Start by listing all the tasks you need or want to accomplish.
- Prioritize your tasks and ensure that critical tasks are scheduled first or depending on your biological primetime.
- Divide your day into blocks to determine the best time for your focused work, open work and shallow work.
- Decide how much time each task should realistically take and assign a specific time slot for it in your calendar.
- Define a clear objective or outcome to achieve by the end of the time period.
- Avoid multitasking, work on the assigned task alone, and stick to the schedule.
- Review, analyze your work speed, and adjust if needed for your next time boxes.

As usual, you need to adapt this technique to your own way of working. I've been speaking with various employees who don't like this technique or find it too difficult to manage alongside their numerous meetings during the day. In this case, blocking off a short amount of time in your calendar in the morning and the afternoon for focused work might be a great way to start.

Applying time boxing enhances concentration, avoids multitasking, reduces procrastination, and improves productivity. It's worth giving it a try – start small and be consistent with it.

IDEA 88

POMODORO TECHNIQUE

The Pomodoro Technique is a popular time management method developed in the late 1980s by Francesco Cirillo. It's named after the Italian word for "tomato," inspired by the tomato-shaped kitchen timer Cirillo used as a university student to track his work sessions.

Cirillo had difficulty completing tasks without experiencing burnout. To overcome this, he decided to challenge himself to concentrate for just ten minutes in order to make progress. To commit to this challenge, he used a tomato-shaped kitchen timer, and the Pomodoro Technique was born.

- Set your timer for 25 minutes (=1 pomodoro), and focus on a single task until the timer rings.
- End work when the timer rings and take a short break (typically 5–10 minutes).
- Start another pomodoro if needed.
- After four pomodoros, take a longer, more restorative 15–30 minute break.

You can combine the Pomodoro Technique with Time Boxing. When organizing your pomodoro or Time Boxing, you may want to plan your hardest task first, making the rest easier.

Other techniques that may suit you better include the Eisenhower Matrix, which categorizes your tasks as urgent, not urgent, important, and not important.

Another technique is the 3/3/3 Method suggested by best-selling author Oliver Burkeman, which involves spending three hours working on an important task, completing three shorter urgent tasks, and dedicating time to three maintenance activities that need attention.

However you choose to handle your workload, it must be structured to avoid multitasking, enhance focus, and increase your productivity.

There are other tricks that can help you work more efficiently and increase your focus with a fun twist:

IDEA
89
FROG OFF

I first heard about this funny technique at the Happiness Woohoo Conference in Denmark.

The idea is simple and can, of course, be adapted:

Showing the image of a frog on your status or having a frog object on your desk gives the direct message that you do not want to be disturbed, and it's your time for immersion and concentration. Let's just say it's quite a direct way of telling someone to go away or leave you alone, but still staying polite.

Depending on your company culture, and especially if your team has a good sense of humor, it can be a fun way to show that you are in your focused time and want to avoid being distracted.

If the "frog off" might not be a good fit for your company's culture, there are other simple ways to express your focused time to others nicely:

➡ Set your status to "Do Not Disturb" on the internal communication platform and be considerate of others who have it enabled. Ensure it's not used excessively to avoid the rule being ignored.

- ➡ Put a sign on your desk or computer to let people know that you don't want to be disturbed during focused work periods. You can use different colored cards or small flags (e.g., green, orange, red) to indicate your availability to be disturbed.
- ➡ Use a do-not-disturb light above your screen or on your desk.
- ➡ Use headphones; people tend to disturb others less if they see them wearing headphones.
- ➡ Use music to boost your concentration levels. Listening to the right music and beats can help reduce mistakes.
- ➡ Use apps to help you stay focused. There are many apps for this; I especially like those with a sustainable impact and reward, such as planting a tree if you don't touch your phone during your focused time.

Scan the QR code to access focus playlists, apps and product examples.

IDEA 90

ADAPT YOUR MEETING CULTURE

On top of having a well-organized meeting with clear objectives, a prepared agenda, a meeting leader, consideration of participants' limitations, an effective summary, and a follow-up, teams and companies need to define a clear meeting culture.

When it comes to desk workers, many of us are jumping from one meeting to the next without much time in between to breathe, think, work, or take a quick break. I often hear from teams I work with that they spend most of their days in meetings, which reduces their productivity, increases their mental fatigue and stress, and causes them to feel they lack progress.

We need to adapt our meeting culture.

Not every meeting requires your presence, not every meeting needs to include cameras and presentations, and not every meeting needs to last for an hour!

By utilizing various meeting formats (online, in-person, standing, walk and talk, phone calls) and keeping meetings shorter, efficiency can be improved.

From 60/30 to 50/25

Adjusting meeting durations from the traditional 60 minutes to 50 minutes, or from 30 minutes to 25 minutes, can enhance efficiency and give participants valuable time between sessions. You can even set the default meeting lengths in your inbox to encourage employees to schedule shorter meetings. These few minutes of "free time" between meetings can allow for a short break, fresh air, doing a task, having a mental pause, or regaining energy; it can make a real difference in employees' well-being.

However, make no mistake, it shouldn't be a quick fix to fit in more meetings. We need to take the problem at the core. If your teams are having too many meetings, address this issue first by, for example, encouraging asynchronous communication, limiting the number of attendees, using collaborative tools to be more efficient, and regularly reviewing the necessity of meetings.

No meeting day

With the rise of remote work and the increase in online meetings, many companies are experimenting with different strategies to help their employees concentrate better. Implementing a "no meeting day" or having official focused hours has often been successful if it's respected and becomes part of the company culture.

On a specific day of the week or during a designated time slot, internal meetings are officially not allowed. The company makes it clear that this time is off-limits for meetings, and if someone schedules a meeting during this time, it's acceptable to politely decline it.

The objective is to provide employees with uninterrupted time to concentrate on deep work, project tasks, and creative processes without the typical disruptions caused by meetings. Making it an official policy and ensuring that everyone, especially leaders, respects it makes it easier for employees to adhere to it and avoid feeling guilty or fearful when refusing a meeting during that designated focused time.

It's not a black-and-white issue. We can consider nuances and make exceptions, but these should be infrequent, and everyone should honor the officially designated focused time. It's clear that this initiative will mainly benefit white-collar workers. If your workforce consists of both white-collar and blue-collar workers, you may want to consider providing other types of benefits for blue-collar workers that focus on improving their physical well-being, such as regular activity breaks.

I have observed many companies, regardless of their size or industry, adapting their meeting culture by reducing meeting times and implementing designated no-meeting periods. While it may seem easier to apply these practices in smaller companies, they can also be effectively implemented in multinational corporations operating across different time zones. The key factors are organization, communication, the integration of these practices into the company's culture, and a true commitment by top leadership.

Adapting your meeting culture will support employees in managing distractions better, preventing burnout, and avoiding falling into an acceleration trap, which is a phenomenon when you are overloaded, multiloaded, and perpetually loaded with no time for recovery.

IDEA 91

GET INSPIRED BY A 4–DAY WEEK

The topic of a 4-day week is finally buzzing in companies!

I have been a big supporter of this idea for many years. You will find, via the QR code, an article I wrote in 2019 about a Danish company that successfully implemented it and an interview from 2023 with the CEO of an IT company in Switzerland who also applied it.

In 2024, I was so passionate about it that I obtained a 4-day-week certification to support companies adopting the 4-day work week.

This topic is gaining traction and it's important to address it in this chapter. Implementing a 4-day work week is a transformative business strategy that focuses on enhancing productivity by working smarter, not longer. Employees who work a 4-day week report feeling happier, less stressed, and less burnt out[7]. While I strongly believe in this concept, I want to emphasize that successful implementation requires careful planning and strategy.

The idea is simple:

- 100% of the pay
- for 80% of the time
- keep productivity at 100%

This is the 100:80:100™ model developed by the 4 Day Week Global Foundation[8].

More and more companies and countries are officially implementing the 4-day week.

The 4 Day Week Global Foundation launched a global campaign and an international pilot program. They have run 4-day-week trials on six continents and can now show significant results in 2024[9]:

- 36% increase in revenue over the previous year
- 42% decrease in employee resignations
- 63% found it easier to attract talent
- 64% reported a reduction in burnout
- 54% reported an increase in work ability

You will find many studies about it on their website, along with top resources to successfully implement a 4-day week. Scan the QR code to find out more.

There is a complete strategy for correctly implementing a 4-day week, and this part deserves a whole book of its own. What I would like to highlight here are the best practices from companies that have implemented a 4-day work week. Even if it's not yet the right time for your company to apply such a shift, being inspired by this format can help all teams become more efficient and work smarter.

Best practices from companies that have implemented a 4-day work week:

➡ They adjust their **meeting culture** by reducing the amount and duration, making their meetings more focused, organized, and efficient.

➡ They **involve the whole team** in brainstorming ways to be more efficient at work and make necessary adaptations.

➡ They use **asynchronous communication**, as employees work at different hours and can access messages at their own pace and preferred location.

➡ They use **social technologies** to share information and improve collaboration.

➡ They handle **administrative work** more effectively.

➡ They leverage **technology** to enhance team productivity (e.g., implementing new project management systems and reducing inefficient processes).

➡ They **train their employees** to use the right tools for productivity and efficiency.

➡ They **optimize and prioritize travel**, especially when visiting clients, to make the most of their travel time.

➡ They **proactively plan** and address challenges to improve efficiency and better manage unexpected situations, saving energy and effort during crises.

➡ They continue to have **regular team gatherings** to nurture work relationships.

➡ They regularly gather **feedback** from employees to check the pulse, collect opinions, and make adjustments if necessary.

➡ They have the **right to disconnect:** "When they are off – they are off." No one will contact them during their day off or holidays. Therefore, having a well-organized workplace and excellent communication between colleagues is crucial.

During my visit to the company IIH Nordic in Denmark in 2019, they shared their formula for ensuring the success of their 4-day week trial:

**Knowledge
+ Tools
+ Behavior
= + Productivity**

- ➡️ **Knowledge:** Employees need to be well-trained and efficient learners.
- ➡️ **Tools:** The company invests in technology and uses the right tools to enhance efficiency. One single tool can significantly reduce the amount of work or people needed for a single task.
- ➡️ **Behavior:** Adapting behaviors and ways of working is crucial for success.

Implementing these elements significantly impacted their employee efficiency and productivity.

Now – do you think your team could implement a 4-day week trial?

Where could you start? What would you need to adapt first?

Implementing a 4-day week takes more than 4 days!

Transitioning from a 5-day work week to a 4-day work week can be a challenging change. However, with thorough preparation, adequate information, support from the right people, and the use of suitable tools, implementing a 4-day week can significantly benefit your company. This change can have a positive impact on your employees, your company's brand, and the overall business.

Nevertheless, it is essential to prioritize improving your company's culture before implementing a 4-day week. Introducing this change in a toxic work environment is unlikely to succeed.

It's important to recognize that there is no one-size-fits-all solution, and the structure of a 4-day week should align with your industry, company culture, and potential for growth.

Implementing a 4-day week might indeed be easier in small or middle-sized companies, but we have seen more and more multinational companies succeed with it. Once you have established a stable and positive team culture, a 4-day work week can enhance your company's performance and act as a significant boost.

IDEA 92

THE "LEARNED HELPFULNESS" METHODOLOGY

Benjamin Delahaye is a busy person. By day, he has a corporate job as President of Online Learning at Education First, and by night, he is a stand-up comic. Both are quite demanding! During a conversation with him, he shared his magic formula for getting things done and being less stressed at work. I couldn't resist sharing it in this book. I believe many of us could find inspiration in it and apply it to our own situations.

Benjamin explains to us his "Learned Helpfulness" methodology:

> *Relax, nothing is under control! – this sentence changed my mindset about stress and work overload.*
>
> *Many goals rely on the actions of others. If you aim to boost sales, ultimately, it's up to the customer to make a purchase. Similarly, increasing the usage of your digital product depends on users choosing to do so. Implementing significant changes in your company will only succeed if thousands of employees embrace the change. These are not invalid goals; in fact, worthy goals have a component that includes someone else's decision.*
>
> *Let's admit that it's frustrating when your success relies on others. As the French philosopher Jean-Paul Sartre once said: "Hell is other people."*
>
> *I used to believe that attending a top MBA school would give me more control and power over my life. However, after graduating, I found myself jobless, crippled with MBA debt, and with the added pressure of having only two weeks to write a wedding speech for my best friend. I realized I was overwhelmed by the fear of not getting what I wanted from others, such as employers offering me a good job and audiences responding positively to my speech at my best friend's wedding. I was unsure of where to start, felt overwhelmed by everything, and lost self-confidence. The fear of failure left me completely powerless and caused me to spiral down into a depression.*

I found it difficult to get off the sofa. I needed to find a solution that suited my poor state of well-being.

I wanted to put to the test the very old saying: "success breeds success," so I made a very simple decision that led to incredible results:

Only give yourself tasks that you are 100% sure you will achieve!

It didn't mean I stopped looking for a job or working on the wedding speech. But my tasks became things I was 100% sure to succeed in: "Today, I will write a three-paragraph cover letter." "Today, I will write for 25 minutes about my best friend." That's it. I decided it would no longer be: "Today you need to find a job" or "Today you will write a hilarious speech."

The magic suddenly unlocked. In one month, I wrote more cover letters than I did in ten months. Because the pressure of the control of other people was removed, I was more productive. I got invited for interviews after only two weeks. My tasks for the interviews were: show up, say these three things about myself, and ask one question. When I removed the subjectivity, the control, and the fear, I became a better version of myself. All of a sudden, in my body, in my voice, there was confidence. I had three job offers after 30 days. And I got a standing ovation at the wedding speech.

*Have you ever heard of **Learned Helplessness**? It's a psychological condition where an individual learns to believe that they are powerless in a situation, even when they have the ability to change or control their circumstances. In short, it's the idea that if you fail at something, you start believing that you will fail at the next thing because you see yourself as a failure. You may be left feeling that no matter what you do or how hard you work, nothing will make a difference.*

*I believe the opposite is true. I call it **Learned Helpfulness**. When you keep accomplishing your tasks, you see yourself as a winner, and suddenly, you start attracting more success into your life, even in areas you don't control. I experienced firsthand that "success breeds success" is true.*

Keep setting goals for yourself, which represent your ambitions and dreams. However, when deciding on tasks, especially when you are feeling over-whelmed or when a goal seems too difficult, only select tasks that you are

100% certain you can accomplish. If there is even a slight chance of failure, reconsider the task. Be firm and unwavering in this approach.

Need another example? Here is a task people might have:

"I need to write a good pitch."

There's a lot of room for failure with that goal. You can't control if the listener will like it, or even if you'll like it yourself. Instead, if you set the goal as "Write a 50-word pitch", that's something you cannot really fail. This will keep you moving forward.

This is a very effective method that has worked for me many times in various aspects of my life, such as in sales, team leadership, organization leadership, public speaking, and comedy writing and performing. Setting and achieving smaller tasks paves the way for accomplishing larger ones. Sometimes, I exceed my goals, sometimes I fall short, and sometimes life surprises me in great and unexpected ways. All these years, this method has kept me productive and active. If I had stressed too much about controlling the achievement of the goal, I would have had paralysis. Instead, I can look back in pride at the end result of what's been accomplished.

You have very little control over your life, but if you use it well, you will be amazed at everything you can achieve.

– Benjamin Delahaye, President of Online Learning, Education First

I believe that Benjamin has a valid point, and I can relate to both phenomena: Learned Helplessness and Learned Helpfulness. Isn't it true that sometimes we feel like everything we do is wrong and that the world is "against us"? I strongly believe that negativity attracts negativity. It's very easy to fall into a dark cycle and lose our self-confidence.

On the other hand, when we succeed at something, it gives us the energy and self-confidence to continue on this path. We often fall into a positive cycle. That's what Benjamin calls Learned Helpfulness. Food for thought, right?

CHAPTER HIGHLIGHTS

✓

We all react to stress differently. What's your own reaction?
Is stress often a friend or mostly an enemy?

✓

Emotions are contagious – especially stress, anxiety and fear – be
conscious of the emotions and behaviors you project around yourself.

✓

Chronic stress activates the hormone cortisol,
known as the "stress hormone," and can have a range
of negative effects on our physical and mental health.

✓

Self-care is crucial to reduce and handle your stress level –
create your own toolbox to help you master stress.

✓

Define your biological primetime
to adapt your workload within different blocks.

✓

We seek distractions to escape dissatisfaction. We need to understand our
triggers to control them and reduce distractions. Track your traction and
distractions and analyze your internal and external triggers.

✓

Working smarter with time management techniques will help you focus
better and avoid being distracted at work.

LET'S TAKE ACTION

➡️ Reflect on your current stress level – on a scale from 1 to 10, how stressed do you feel lately?

➡️ What actions could you take to improve your self-care?

➡️ What will be your next step to work smarter?

Remember to download the Stress Management Toolbox template by scanning the QR code for this chapter. You can personalize the toolbox.

Access additional resources by scanning the QR code.

YOUR THOUGHTS
YOUR JOURNEY

Capture your insights, ideas, and action steps as you make this journey your own.

10

FOSTERING A FEELING OF ACHIEVEMENT

Feeling of Achievement –
A Cornerstone to Feeling Good
at Work

Do you feel like you actually achieve something at work?

During one of the programs I led for an international company, I had an interesting session with an employee who had a strong feeling of not achieving much at work. Although she would spend time jumping from one meeting to another, answering tons of urgent emails, finishing PowerPoint presentations, and finalizing the budget, she still said she didn't feel she had achieved much that day. You might relate, as her situation is not rare – I hear similar stories from many employees I work with.

And usually, how do we feel at the end of such a day? Tired, empty, with no energy and no sense of progress – which might not be rational at all as we usually accomplish more than we think!

We often juggle multiple tasks throughout the day, yet still feel like we're not making meaningful progress.

This sense of stagnation arises because we tend to focus on what's left unfinished rather than recognizing what we've accomplished. Sometimes, it's also because we lack clarity on the purpose of our work or miss the recognition and praise that reinforces our efforts. When these factors combine, the feeling of underachievement becomes even more pronounced.

When we feel like we're not progressing and haven't achieved anything, big or small, it can lead to frustration, stress, lack of motivation, and disengagement—basically a terrible combo to foster positivity at work.

On the other hand, when employees experience moments of achievement, it cultivates a culture of success and positivity that resonates throughout the organization. According to a study by Gallup[1], recognition for achievements at work can increase employee engagement, reduce turnover rates, and foster a more cooperative team environment. This sense of success contributes to a virtuous cycle where achievements motivate further achievements, setting a foundation for a resilient and adaptive work culture. It sounds like the "Learned Helplessness" method explained by Benjamin in Chapter 9 – right?

I specifically chose to use the term "***feeling*** of achievement" instead of "sense of achievement," which might be more common in the workplace. This is to emphasize the emotional aspect and focus on the subjective experience associated with achieving something.

As explained in Chapter 1, building good relationships and cultivating a feeling of achievement within teams are essential pillars of building a positive work culture.

The following factors will influence and cultivate your feeling of achievement:

- Receiving recognition and praise for your good work
- Having a healthy feedback culture that allows you to learn and grow
- Working on personal development and learning new skills
- Aligning skills with tasks to be more in the flow (losing track of time when working on a task you enjoy doing)
- Setting clear goals that are achievable
- Being well organized and using project management systems to track progress
- Being empowered with autonomy to feel responsible and pride in your work
- Feeling that your work is valuable and useful, and understanding its impact. Finding meaning and purpose in your role and tasks (aligning with personal values)
- Feeling proud of your contributions to the company

If you feel that you are lacking in any of these areas, please ensure you complete the "take action" section at the end of this chapter to reflect on what you can implement to enhance your feeling of achievement.

In this chapter, I want to emphasize simple strategies for celebrating your achievements at work and increasing the visibility of your workload. Both will significantly improve your feeling of achievement. The previous chapters should have already helped you enhance your feedback culture, be more efficient and focused, and discover more meaning, purpose, and joy in your work.

Let's explore some simple, actionable strategies to recognize achievements and increase their visibility within your team.

Celebrate All Achievements – Not Just the Big Ones!

Celebrating both small and big wins at work boosts team morale and motivation, and provides employees with tangible recognition of their efforts and success. It reinforces positive behaviors, enhances job satisfaction, and fosters a positive work culture.

It also builds a sense of community and belonging, as team celebrations bring individuals together, strengthening bonds and improving teamwork. In summary, taking the time to celebrate wins can lead to increased productivity, enhanced employee engagement, and a more harmonious work environment.

CELEBRATE ALL YOUR WINS

NOT JUST THE BIGGEST ONES

IDEA 93

There are many ways to make your successes visible, and I will provide several examples in this section. First, it's crucial to recognize the importance of celebrating all types of victories within your team, not just the major ones. Acknowledging smaller achievements reinforces a culture of progress, helps team members feel valued, and fosters a sense of belonging. This recognition keeps motivation high, as individuals feel that their efforts are noticed, which in turn fuels ongoing productivity and engagement over the long term.

We shouldn't wait for the end-of-year review, the company town hall announcing the employee of the month, or an official team event to celebrate a new accomplishment.

Having a visual tool such as a success wall for celebrating achievements will help maintain motivation, positivity, and pride in teams. It provides public acknowledgment and makes team members feel valued and appreciated.

You can use different formats for your success wall:

- Create a physical success wall in a prominent spot accessible to all team members (common room, entrance, cafeteria, entrance hall, etc.).
- Use interactive elements to make the wall more visual and fun. It can include pictures of the team or employees, thank-you cards from clients, or any visuals that represent the win to celebrate (however small).
- Make a digital wall for remote or hybrid teams using interactive platforms such as Trello, Padlet, or your intranet page.
- Celebrate all types of wins– not only professional milestones but also personal achievements if appropriate, such as winning a sports competition, mastering a new skill, or getting married.
- Add customer feedback to this wall or even create a wall specifically for it – many employees are not directly in touch with the end customer,

and it might reinforce the meaning and impact of their work by knowing about the positive outcomes.

➡ Announce the "Happy Projects": add all successful projects/products on the board and explain how they were successful – it's a good way to reflect on what went well and why.

Choose a name that resonates with your team – whether it's the Success Wall, Wall of Wins, Champion's Wall, or Victory Lane. Find what aligns with your culture and make it a symbol of achievement!

Recognizing our achievements reinforces the behaviors and strategies that contribute to success. Equally important is reflecting on our mistakes, as it provides valuable insights and learning opportunities for future improvement. Both practices are essential for continuous personal and professional growth, fostering a culture of learning and resilience.

IDEA 94

THE POWER OF A TEAM SHOUT-OUT

It is common for companies to celebrate the "Employee of the Month," but this practice can be perceived as both positive and negative. While it is a great way to recognize an individual's performance and outstanding work, it tends to focus solely on individuals rather than teamwork, potentially leading to jealousy or resentment among other employees.

Companies can get creative by adding a fun twist to the traditional "Employee of the Month" award by introducing special titles instead: "Problem Solver of the Month," "Creative Queen or King," "The Great Team Player," "Presentation Pro of the Year," "Mental Health Advocate" or "Positivity Powerhouse"! Find the ones that align with your employees and culture.

Fun trophies or certificates can be given to make the event more enjoyable, memorable, and with less pressure around the "Employee of the Month." Giving this kind of award can be a great opportunity to start a conversation and emphasize best-practice sharing. Ask the award recipients to share their best tips for presenting as a pro, taking care of their mental health, or how they foster a positive mindset.

It's also important to consider that not everyone enjoys public recognition. Depending on the culture or the individual, standing on stage in front of the whole company to receive an award might be challenging for some people. Recognizing the entire team might have a better effect.

Giving a shout-out to the entire team to showcase their success is a powerful way to highlight the team's work. This can be done on the company's internal or external communication platforms, through the newsletter, intranet, social media, special event, or a company-wide email to enhance the team's visibility and public recognition.

Highlighting our wins is great; however, developing a positive work culture is not only about highlighting the good. It's also about managing challenges or difficult situations in an effective way.

IDEA 95

OOPS BOARD TO ACCEPT & OWN FAILURES

Let's be honest – everyone makes mistakes at work, and that's both normal and essential for learning and growth. However, accepting our mistakes or failures can be tough. While we do learn and improve from them, it's important not to underestimate the emotional toll. Failure can leave us feeling lonely, guilty, and demotivated, and it's often hard to see the positive side right away.

Owning our "oops" (as I like to call them) can take a while. In certain situations, we need to take the time to process it.

Remember:

When we acknowledge our difficult feelings, we get through them with less intensity!

Our frustrations will help us take action, adapt, and change something that doesn't work.

I like this common approach to owning our failures:

- **Pause:** Take a moment to pause and reflect – acknowledge your emotions
- **Process:** Reflect on it, process the details and impacts
- **Plan:** With a rational mindset, plan a course of action if needed
- **Proceed:** Reframe, adapt and take action

It is indeed possible to create a positive spin on the process of learning from failures, making it an integral and proactive part of team development and organizational growth.

3 Ways to make the most out of failures at work:

- **Ask relevant questions in teams to normalize mistakes and encourage open dialogue:**
  - *What can we change going forward to avoid repeating the mistake?*
  - *Is there a decision or action you would change if you had the chance? Why?*
  - *Can you share a situation where things didn't turn out as you expected? What would you do differently next time?*
  - *What lessons have you learned from your last project that didn't meet the goals?*
- **Create an "Oops" board:** Like the success wall previously explained, you can do the same to celebrate and announce the things that didn't work out! As a team, you can, for example, use such a board to visualize the products of your company that didn't go to the market, or a project that failed. Reflect on the why and on the learnings.
- **Keep a failure journal:** Write down the things that didn't work out as you wished, the things that you had to drop, or the mistakes you made. It's a great way to vent, and it will help you to analyze, learn, and grow. Don't ruminate, but understand the mistakes or challenges better.

When we share what we've learned with others in the company, all can benefit, and we foster an environment of openness, transparency, and continuous improvement.

Especially with these kinds of initiatives, we need to have leaders walking the talk. If leaders do not embrace their mistakes, employees will not feel safe being transparent and owning theirs.

Leaders should model the behavior they wish to see. When leaders handle their errors with integrity and openness, it sets a powerful precedent for the entire organization.

IDEA 96

COFFEE TIME WITH THE CEO

I have seen this initiative rising in companies since the COVID-19 pandemic. During lockdowns, many companies offered the opportunity to have an online coffee time with their CEO or someone from the leadership team. This casual setting allows for candid dialogue, bridging the gap between executive leadership and employees at all levels.

Employees often ask questions about upcoming projects, goals, long-term vision, people development, and specific restructuring. It helps them gain a better understanding of the company's direction, fulfilling their sense of belonging and achievement.

It's also a great way for executives to connect with employees, assess how they feel, gather firsthand insights, and address current concerns. The CEO might ask for feedback and suggestions while also taking the pulse of employees' overall well-being.

What to talk about during a coffee break with the CEO?

The main topics could be:

- Vision and strategy
- Company structure
- Culture and people

- The latest news, launch, or challenge
- Employee feedback and suggestions
- Best practice sharing
- Personal stories

For a long-term impact:

- Try to have an open agenda to encourage genuine interaction.
- Make it regular and not just once a year.
- Make it interactive using technology to ask questions and collect answers or ideas.
- Follow up to reinforce the effectiveness of sessions and show employees the importance of their input.

The success of "coffee time with the CEO" will depend on the CEO's reputation, the company's culture, and everyone's openness. If people don't feel safe asking questions, don't trust the leadership, or find this initiative like a joke, it will backfire!

While connecting with leadership is important for building bonds and understanding long-term vision, maintaining visibility of daily tasks is also crucial for enhancing your sense of achievement at work.

We get so focused on what we haven't done that we forget to count the things we have! Let's explore some daily strategies for tracking progress.

Visualize Your Progress at Work

Visualizing progress at work offers a clear sense of direction and accomplishment. It enables individuals and teams to see tangible results from their efforts. This continuous awareness boosts motivation and reinforces a growth mindset.

IDEA 97

Daily check-in rituals are brief meetings to align team members, encourage communication, and track task progress. They help to maintain accountability, discuss your daily goals, allow swift work adjustments, and strengthen team cohesion. Typically short and focused, these check-ins are held regularly at the start of the workday.

It's essential to foster an environment where everyone feels safe to answer these questions honestly. Trust is key for this ritual to succeed.

Here are some ideas of questions that can be asked during these check-ins:

- *Describe in two words how you are feeling today*
  To support emotional and mental health awareness and adjust workload if possible.

- *What are you planning to work on today?*
  To have a clear plan, be organized, and set clear expectations for the day.

- *Are there any blockers or challenges you're facing? Do you need support?*
  To request help or resources if needed, prevent delays and be proactive.

- *What's one thing that could make your day easier or more productive?*
  To encourage finding the flow state and being more focused.

- *What do you feel excited about today?*
  To boost team morale, encourage developing a positive mindset, and identify motivators.

Depending on the situation, you might start by picking only three or doing them all. Once the team is used to this ritual, it will be faster and more efficient, and you will not want to miss it!

Remember to practice your listening skills. Employees need to feel heard and valued. This ritual will enhance collaboration, trust, and communication if done well. Refer back to Chapter 6 to apply the L-I-S-T-E-N method!

If you are not regularly in touch with your team or not part of a specific team, these questions can also help as self-reflection to start your day properly.

The way we start and end our working day has a huge influence on our holistic well-being.

Finishing your day on a positive note is as important as how you start it.

IDEA
98

DAILY
CHECK-OUT RITUAL

How you end your day is critical! The first and last impressions of your day will have a huge impact on your mood, attitude, and view of your work. Ending your day on a good note will significantly increase your feeling of achievement and overall fulfillment and get you ready with a more peaceful mindset for the next day.

Keep in mind that end-of-day reflection is not just about tracking achievements – it's a vital step in maintaining your well-being and reducing work-related stress.

Choose from these self-reflection questions or actions for your check-out ritual:

- *Today, I achieved this …*
  Evaluate your to-do list and highlight important or difficult tasks you have achieved.

- *Today, I especially enjoyed doing …*
  Reflect on the tasks you enjoyed or the part of the job you like.

- *My highlight of the day is …*
  Reduce your negativity bias and reflect on the positive things of the day (something that made you smile, a small or big win, a nice time with a colleague, an email from a client, etc.)

- *Tomorrow, I will first …*
  Review your schedule for the next day and adapt your agenda or priorities if needed. It will help you start your day more organized and less stressed.

- **Get closure to be able to switch off**

  Finish a key task or send the emails you've wanted to send all day. Clean and organize your desk for the next day, take a deep breath, and it's time to go home!

Leaving behind our stress and mental workload at the office can be challenging; this practice encourages you to disconnect from work and create a clear boundary between your working hours and your personal time at home.

IDEA 99

TRANSFORM YOUR TO-DO LIST INTO A TA-DA LIST

Another way to better visualize your daily achievements is to transform your to-do list into a "ta-da" list! (and please read it with a "ta-daaaaa!!!" tone and attitude!)

Rather than concentrating on tasks that remain unfinished, a ta-da list highlights everything you've already accomplished. So, when you wonder, *"How did I spend my day?"* you can simply check your ta-da list – and you'll likely discover you've achieved more than you initially realized.

There are many ways to create a ta-da list:

- Use and twist the Kanban board model (to-do/doing/done) and replace "done" with "ta-da!" to celebrate every little victory as you track your progress. After all, every task completed deserves a mini celebration!
- As you complete an important task, write it down on a clean piece of paper and complete your ta-da list throughout the day.
- Highlight in a specific color your completed tasks to visualize your ta-das.
- I personally often add a smiley after crossing an important task on my to-do list – it's my way to visualize and celebrate my ta-das!

However big or small your ta-das are, documenting them can be a great motivator and a fun tool to develop a feeling of achievement.

IDEA 100

SPICE UP YOUR END-OF-YEAR REVIEW

Beyond the typical end-of-year or mid-year review—where we usually discuss major achievements, overall performance, give and receive feedback, and plan for the months ahead—let's consider adding elements that foster emotional connection.

Try adding some of these questions to your next end-of-year review:

- **What is your definition of happiness at work, and how close are you to it?**
  Refer to Chapter 1 for a reminder. You can open and develop the discussion with other questions such as: *"How's your happiness level lately?"* *"What are you doing to get closer to your definition of happiness at work?"* *"Where do you need support?"*

- **How was your holistic well-being this year?**
  Refer to Chapter 3 for more inspiration.
  Ask other questions such as: **"***How would you rate your current mental/physical well-being?"* or *"What's one thing that supports your well-being that you want to continue doing next year?"*

- **What were your highlights of the year?**
  This is a great way to remember and realize everything achieved, to feel successful, and to boost self-confidence! Also, it's an opportunity to celebrate these highlights.

- **What do you want to say goodbye to?**
  The end of the year is also a great way to let go and accept! It can be a feeling they don't want to have anymore, or maybe something they are holding on to that maybe they don't need anymore (e.g., the feeling of being a perfectionist or not good enough, too much pressure, or a project that didn't go well and got on their nerves way too much).

- **How do you want to feel this coming year?**
  What kind of colleague/leader do you want to be? These kinds of questions will make them reflect on where they are now and where they want to go next year (not as a destination but more as a state of being).

In this chapter, we have explored various ways to recognize one's achievements during a working day, create a feeling of belonging and coherence within a team, and motivate oneself and one's colleagues. All these techniques aim to increase positive emotions about the work that has been done or the tasks ahead of us.

Indeed, it requires discipline to perform some of these techniques before, during, or after a busy day. Regardless, the long-term results, ranging from more individual motivation to high-delivering teams, outweigh the effort by far.

CHAPTER HIGHLIGHTS

✔

We might feel that we didn't achieve much because we most probably focus on what we still have to do and ignore what we've accomplished.

✔

When we feel like we're not progressing and haven't achieved anything, big or small, it can lead to frustration, stress, lack of motivation, and disengagement.

✔

When employees experience moments of achievement,
it cultivates a culture of success and positivity
that resonates throughout the organization.

✔

The first and last impressions of your day will have a huge impact on your mood, attitude, and view of your work.

✔

Fostering good relationships and cultivating a feeling of achievement within teams are important pillars of building a positive work culture.

LET'S TAKE ACTION

➡ Do you feel you're achieving things at work?
If yes, what methods are you using to visualize your achievements? Is it enough?
Otherwise, consider what you could do to work more effectively, make progress, or recognize your accomplishments.

➡ Start a ta-da list and analyze all the small things you achieved during the day – how do you feel about it? Is it an initiative you'll try to implement in your daily work?

➡ Reflect with your colleagues/team on what is already in place to make the team's progress visible and what can be implemented to increase the sense of achievement in your team.

Access additional resources by scanning the QR code.

YOUR THOUGHTS
YOUR JOURNEY

Capture your insights, ideas, and action steps as you make this journey your own.

FINAL THOUGHTS

Creating and sustaining a positive work culture is a beautiful journey. As you have explored through the 100 ideas in this book, a thriving work environment requires consistent, intentional effort from everyone within the organization.

A positive work culture is built on the foundations of shared responsibility, continuous growth, and a genuine commitment to the well-being of each individual.

Throughout this book, we've examined the importance of workplace happiness, the impact of emotional intelligence, the role of an effective employee experience, and the power of meaningful relationships. It has become clear that a positive work culture goes beyond superficial gestures; it involves creating an environment where people feel respected, valued, and empowered.

Embracing positivity doesn't mean ignoring challenges or difficult situations and emotions – it means cultivating resilience, empathy, and a solution-oriented mindset that can help teams navigate challenges together.

Indeed, leaders play an important role in shaping this environment through authentic and positive leadership that resonates with employees and inspires them to behave and perform at their best. Feedback, another cornerstone of a healthy work culture, can help individuals grow when delivered with empathy and respect.

Ultimately, managing stress, boosting focus, and fostering a feeling of achievement enables each person to contribute to a culture of positivity and productivity. When employees can work effectively and reflect on their work with a sense of fulfillment, it fuels motivation and drives engagement.

As you embark on this journey, remember that small, consistent actions can make a lasting impact. It's not about implementing everything at once; it's about finding the initiative, the tool, or the strategy that makes sense for you, your team, and your workflow at a given point in time.

Remember to scan the QR code for fresh resources, expert insights, and regular updates to help you stay up-to-date and have a sustainable impact!

This book is your toolbox to empower you and the ones around you.

Every time you take a step toward creating a positive work culture, you're contributing to a movement that truly makes a difference.

Your actions will create ripple effects of positivity that you'll spread in your workplace and beyond!

Access additional resources by scanning the QR code.

IDEAS INDEX

THE AUTHOR'S STORY

They used to call me:

The Happy Frenchie!

I left my hometown in the South of France at the age of 19 to work in England, improve my English, and chase my big dreams. My journey then took me to Vancouver, Canada, and Geneva, before finally arriving in Zurich, Switzerland. In every company I worked for, I brought the same positive energy—the "Happy Frenchie Energy."

However, I have to admit that there were times when I lost it, and it was painful.

Frustrations in the workplace are common—I've experienced them many times. From dealing with toxic leaders and unhelpful colleagues to losing the meaning of my work, sitting in meetings filled with negativity, or even facing a manager in "bullying mode," I've seen how these frustrations impacted my motivation, engagement, and overall performance.

At one point, I completely lost my positive attitude and my smile and found myself stuck in a negative cycle. My happiness at work was gone. Until my friend made me realize I needed to find happiness again. That was the turning point when I decided to dive deeper into the insights of top experts and get various certifications in positive psychology, well-being, neuroplasticity, emotional intelligence, stress management, and change management.

It became my mission to bring more awareness to companies and to prove that with a positive attitude, we can work much better. Frustrations can be minimized when we all know how to act with more positivity. I envisioned transforming these frustrations and negativity into more happiness and positivity.

Today, I am an expert in Positive Work Culture, a TEDx speaker, and a certified Chief Well-being Officer and Chief Happiness Officer, supporting teams and leaders worldwide in fostering a human-centric culture where everyone can be at their best.

Let's be changemakers together to inspire individuals to become the best versions of themselves and help companies create environments where teams flourish. Join me!

Let's connect and follow me by scanning my social media QR code.

Check also my website for more info: aurelielitynski.com

WORDS OF APPRECIATION

We did it!

You, me, and this book—we've shared some time together, and now I would like to give a standing ovation to everyone who made this experience possible.

First and foremost, **to you, dear reader**: Thank you for picking up this book, for your curiosity, and for believing in the power of positivity at work. Whether you have been reading this book on your lunch break, between meetings, or curled up on the couch, know that I am incredibly grateful for your time and attention. You are the reason why this book exists. Now you have in your hands many ideas for enhancing your own happiness and fostering a positive work culture around you.

The other two people who deserve my deepest gratitude are **my husband Tytus and my dear friend Ana.** Let me share a brief story about how this book came to life and their crucial roles in it.

Ana was the first person to inspire me to write a book, and she has encouraged me for many years. As one of my best friends, author of two books, and a writing coach, it was hard for me to resist her idea of writing my own book. After a long walk on a rainy Easter Day in 2024, I finally agreed with Ana that I would start writing my book. She had been trying to motivate me to do this for four years. The concept was in my mind for so long; I knew exactly what I wanted to share and how I envisioned the book.

When I returned home and announced to my husband that I would finally begin writing, he challenged me to complete the first draft within four months. Knowing me well, he realized that I needed a deadline and some pressure to finish. Consequently, within approximately six months and with his endless support managing everything around, I had my very first draft ready. Sometimes, all it takes is a little push... and a lot of support!

I am profoundly grateful to both of them for believing in me and supporting me through my many ups and downs. They truly deserve a medal!

To my wonderful friends— especially Marie, Bianca, Zsofia, Nadia and Mon-ika—thank you for being incredibly supportive. You were always willing to brainstorm with me, read chapters, and provide your mental support. Your patience and love kept me going.

To my very first beta readers: Manouchka, Joti, Becca, Charlotte, Eva, Eric, Ludovic and Igaël. Thank you for your honesty, encouragement, and thoughtful notes that pushed this book to be its best.

I also want to deeply thank all **the fantastic leaders and experts** featured in this book for sharing their stories and experiences with me. Additionally, I extend my appreciation **to all my clients** with whom I have worked over the years; their in-sights and best practices have greatly contributed to the foundation of this book.

To all the experts I have learned from, including Laurie Santos, Martin Selig-man, Tal Ben-Shahar, Simon Sinek, Rick Hanson, Daniel Goleman, Nir Eyal, and Jim Kwik. For years, your work has inspired me, shaped my understanding, and provided the foundation for many ideas in this book. Thank you for sharing your wisdom so generously—it has been a guiding light on my journey.

Also, thank you **to my illustrator**, Jun Han Chin, for bringing my ideas to life with fun and meaningful illustrations; **to my designer**, Francesca Poggi from Bright Lines, for her creativity and vision in making this book both beautiful and engaging; and **to my photographer**, Mafe from Mafe Photo, for capturing my author portrait beautifully.

I want to extend my gratitude **to my publishing agency**, Gareth from Auth-oright, and my editorial team, Dave and Beth, for their invaluable support.

And finally, to my two daughters, Amelia and Alicia, who make me a better person every day, and who had the patience of having a stressed and busy mum writing a book in her office upstairs. This book is also for you, to help you realize that in the future, at work, you can—and should—be happy and spread positivity around you. Always remember that our emotions are contagious. Make good use of this throughout your lives.

Merci to everyone!

Aurelie Litynski

REFERENCES

Chapter 1

1   Affect and Creativity at Work – Teresa M. Amabile, Sigal G. Barsade, Jennifer S. Mueller, and Barry M. Staw – Administrative Science Quarterly *https://web.mit.edu/curhan/www/docs/Articles/15341_Readings/Affect/Amabile.pdf*
    The Benefits of Frequent Positive Affect: Does Happiness Lead to Success? – Sonja Lyubomirsky, Laura King, and Ed Diener – Psychological Bulletin *https://eric.ed.gov/?id=EJ735265*
    Happiness and Productivity – Andrew J.Oswald, Eugenio Proto, and Daniel Sgroi – Warwick University *https://wrap.warwick.ac.uk/id/eprint/63228/7/WRAP_Oswald_681096.pdf*

2   The Happy Secret to Better Work – Shan Achor – TEDX Talk *https://www.ted.com/talks/shawn_achor_the_happy_secret_to_better_work/*

3   Employee Wellbeing, Productivity and Firm Performance – Christian Krekel, George Ward, Jan-Emmanuel De Neve – LSE –*https://cep.lse.ac.uk/pubs/download/dp1605.pdf*

4   Book The Service Profit Chain – James L. Heskett, W. Earl Sasser, Jr Leonard A, Schleisinger

5   Highly Engaged but Burned Out: Intra-Individual Profiles in the US Workforce – Julia Moeller, Zorana Ivcevic, Arielle E. White, Jochen I. Menges, Marc A. Brackett – Career Development International *https://www.emerald.com/insight/content/doi/10.1108/CDI-12-2016-0215/full/html*

6   The Science of Well-Being – Laurie Santos – Online Course Yale University *https://www.drlauriesantos.com/science-well-being*

7   What Makes a Good Life? Lessons From the Longest Study on Happiness – Robert Waldinger – TED Talk
    https://www.ted.com/talks/robert_waldinger_what_makes_a_good_life_lessons_from_the_longest_study_on_happiness

Chapter 2

1   The Negativity Bias: Why the Bad Stuff Sticks – Margaret Jaworski – HealthCentral *https://www.healthcentral.com/mental-health/negativity-bias*

2   The Positive Neuroplasticity Training – Rick Hanson *https://rickhanson.com/*

3   Will Bowen – *https://complaintfree.willbowen.com/*

Chapter 3

1   Future of Mental Health Report Survey – Forrester *https://join.modernhealth.com/future-of-mental-health-2021-report-forrester.html*

2   Happiest Companies Better in Multiple Measures of Firm Performance – University of Oxford and the Well-Being Research Centre *https://wellbeing.hmc.ox.ac.uk/news/stock-market-performance/*

3   A Meta-Analysis of the Relative Contribution of Leadership Styles to Followers' Mental Health – Diego Montano, Joyce Elena Schleu, and Joachim Hüffmeier – Journal of Leadership & Organizational Studies *https://cdn.thehuddle-aws.com/uploads/tenants/8201/202307/124911-a_montano-et-al-2022-a-meta-analysis-of-the-relative-contribution-of-leadership-styles-to-followers-mental-health.pdf*

4   The 17 Sustainable Development Goals – UN Department of Economic and Social Affairs *https://sdgs.un.org/goals*

5   Well-Being at Work Survey 2023 – Deloitte *https://www2.deloitte.com/us/en/insights/topics/talent/workplace-well-being-research.html*

6   The 5 Essentials for Workplace Mental Health and Well-Being. U.S. Surgeon General's Framework for Workplace Mental Health & Well-Being *https://www.hhs.gov/surgeongeneral/priorities/workplace-well-being/index.html*

7   Measuring Workplace Well-being – Jan-Emmanuel De Neve and George Ward – University of Oxford and the Well-Being Research Centre *https://wellbeing.hmc.ox.ac.uk/wp-content/uploads/2023/05/2303-WP-Measuring-Workplace-Wellbeing-DOI.pdf*

8   National Institute for Health and care Excellence (NICE). Mental wellbeing at work (NICE Guideline NG212)

9   Well-Being at Work Survey 2023 – Deloitte *https://www2.deloitte.com/us/en/insights/topics/talent/workplace-well-being-research.html*

Chapter 4

1   Gallup's Perspective on Creating an Exceptional Onboarding Journey for New Employees *https://www.gallup.com/workplace/247076/onboarding-new-employees-perspective-paper.aspx*

2   BambooHR Onboarding Statistics Reveal What New Employees Really Want in 2023 *https://www.bamboohr.com/resources/assets/ebooks/10-onboarding-statistics-2023.pdf*

Chapter 5

1   The Harvard Study of Adult Development – The Harvard Gazette *https://news.harvard.edu/gazette/story/2023/02/work-out-daily-ok-but-how-socially-fit-are-you/*

2   The Broaden-and-Build Theory of Positive Emotions – Barbara L Fredrickson *https://pubmed.ncbi.nlm.nih.gov/15347528/*

3   Positive Impact, Creativity, and Innovative Behavior at Work: The Mediating Role of Basic Needs Satisfaction – Konstantinos Papachristopoulos, Marc-Antoine Gradito Dubord, Florence Jauvin, Jacques Forest, and Patrick Coulombe *https://www.mdpi.com/2076-328X/13/12/984*

Chapter 6

1   Emotional Intelligence and Job Performance: A Meta-Analysis – Jaroslaw Grobelny, Patrycja Radke, and Daria Paniotova – International Journal of Work Organization and Emotion *https://www.inderscience.com/offers.php?id=115620*

2   A Meta-Analysis of Emotional Intelligence and Work Attitudes – Chao Miao, Ronald Humphrey, and Shanshan Qian – Lancaster University *https://eprints.lancs.ac.uk/id/eprint/83719/*

3   Daniel Goleman *https://www.danielgoleman.info/*

Chapter 7

1 A Meta-Analysis of the Relative Contribution of Leadership Styles to Followers' Mental Health – Diego Montano, Joyce Elena Schleu, and Joachim Hüffmeier – Journal of Leadership & Organizational Studies *https://cdn.thehuddle-aws.com/uploads/tenants/8201/202307/124911-a_montano-et-al-2022-a-meta-analysis-of-the-relative-contribution-of-leadership-styles-to-followers-mental-health.pdf*

Chapter 8

1 Preparing the Self for Team Entry: How Relational Affirmation Improves Team Performance –Julia J. Lee, Francesca Gino, Daniel M. Cable, and Bradley R. Staats *https://positiveorgs.bus.umich.edu/articles/preparing-the-self-for-team-entry-how-relational-affirmation-improves-team-performance/*

2 Employee Engagement Statistics From Across the Globe – Workleap *https://Workleap.Com/Blog/State-Employee-Engagement-Guide/*

Chapter 9

1 80% Of Employees Report "Productivity Anxiety" and Lower Well-Being In New Study – The American Institute of Stress – *https://www.stress.org/news/80-of-employees-report-productivity-anxiety-and-lower-well-being-in-new-study/*

2 Sleep and Emotional Processing – Daniela Tempesta, Valentina Socci, Luigi De Gennaro, Michele Ferrara – Science Direct *https://www.sciencedirect.com/science/article/abs/pii/S1087079217301533*

3 The Best Sleep Tips – Dr Els van der Helm – LinkedIn Newsletter *https://www.linkedin.com/pulse/catching-up-sleep-do-dont-dr-els-van-der-helm-vhtje/*

4 Give Your Ideas Some Legs: The Positive Effect of Walking on Creative Thinking – Marily Oppezzo and Daniel L. Schwartz – Stanford University *https://www.apa.org/pubs/journals/releases/xlm-a0036577.pdf*

5 Workplace Distractions Statistics: Problems and Solutions in 2024 – TeamStage *https://teamstage.io/workplace-distractions-statistics/* Multitasking: Switching costs – American Psychological Association (APA) *https://www.apa.org/topics/research/multitasking*

6 Nir Eyal's Book Indistractable and online course The 4 Keys To Indistractable Focus.

7 How the 4 Day Work Week Can Improve Employees' Mental Well-Being – 4 Day Week Global Foundation *https://www.4dayweek.com/news-posts/mental-health*

8 The 100:80:100™ Rule – 4 Day Week Global Foundation *https://www.4dayweek.com/news-posts/100-80-100-rule*

9 4 Day Week Global Foundation *https://www.4dayweek.com/research*

Chapter 10

1 The Human-Centered Workplace: Building Organizational Cultures That Thrive – Gallup and Workhuman *https://www.gallup.com/analytics/472658/workplace-recognition-research.aspx*